AVRO
LANCASTER

1941 onwards (all marks)

Published in April 2008

A catalogue record for this book is available from the British Library

ISBN 978 1 84425 463 7

Library of Congress control no. 2007943094

Published by Haynes Publishing, Sparkford, Yeovil, Somerset BA22 7JJ, UK
Tel: 01963 442030 Fax: 01963 440001
Int. tel: +44 1963 442030 Int. fax: +44 1963 440001
E-mail: sales@haynes.co.uk
Website: www.haynes.co.uk

Haynes North America Inc.
861 Lawrence Drive, Newbury Park,
California 91320, USA

Printed and bound in Great Britain by
J. H. Haynes & Co. Ltd, Sparkford

WARNING
While every attempt has been made throughout this book to emphasise the safety aspects of working on, restoring and flying a Lancaster, the authors and publishers accept no liability whatsoever for any damage, injury or loss resulting from the use of this book.

Acknowledgements

Gathering the material for this manual would have been impossible without the enthusiastic support of so many within the world of active Lancaster preservation:

Battle of Britain Memorial Flight – OC BBMF Squadron Leader Al Pinner MBE, Flight Lieutenant Ed Straw, BBMF 'Bomber Leader' Squadron Leader Stuart Reid, BBMF 'Navigation Leader' Squadron Leader Jeff Hesketh, Flight Engineer Squadron Leader Ian Morton, Flight Lieutenant Jack Hawkins, Warrant Officer Dick Harmer, Public Relations Officer Jeanette O'Connell, Jim Stewart and Di Holland.

RAF Museum London – Development Manager Rebecca Dalley for her valued assistance in supplying photographs and posters from the museum's collection.

Aeroplane Monthly for kind permission to reproduce the cutaway drawing of the Lancaster that appears on the cover and on pp38-9.

Lincolnshire Aviation Heritage Centre – Fred Panton MBE, Harold Panton, Ian Hickling, Andrew Panton and Mark Fletcher.

Canadian Warplane Heritage Museum – Don Schofield; Mark Watt and Doug Fisher of Warbird Depot (www.warbirddepot.com) for kindly supplying pictures of the Canadian Lancaster.

Haynes Publishing – Jonathan Falconer, Steve Rendle and James Robertson for their patience with the authors throughout the production process of this book – it is important to remember that without them what you see before you would not exist!

Also much appreciation goes to Bruce Irvine of Classic Aircraft Maintenance for words and pictures appertaining to PA474's latest major overhaul, and to Dale and Andrea Featherby for the beautiful air-to-air photograph of it in its current *Phantom of the Ruhr* paint scheme.

And last, but by no means least, Louise Blackah, who worked tirelessly to assist with the preparation of the technical content and made sure Paul kept on track with this project when he wasn't 'fixing' the Lancaster; and Clare Cotter, who typed up manuscripts when her husband was away looking at aeroplanes.

To all of these contributors, the authors sincerely offer their grateful thanks.

COVER CUTAWAY: Avro Lancaster BI by J. H. Clark ARAeS (courtesy of *Aeroplane Monthly*/www.aeroplanemonthly.com)

AVRO
LANCASTER

1941 onwards (all marks)

Haynes

RAF

◎ROYAL Battle of Britain
AIR FORCE Memorial Flight
OFFICIAL PRODUCT

Owners' Workshop Manual

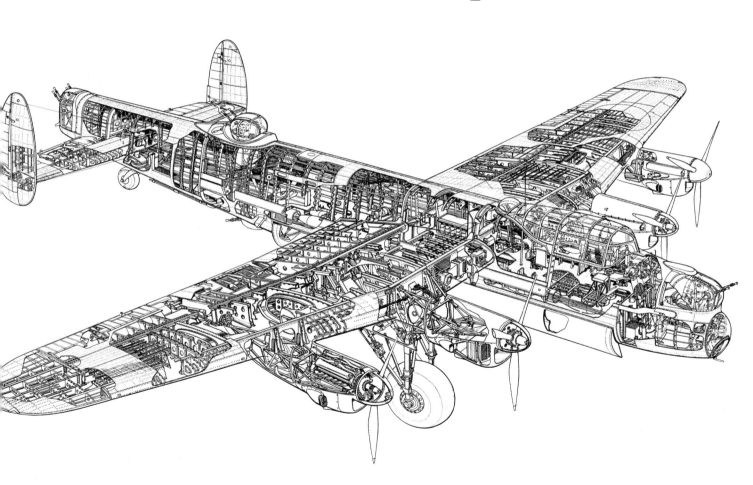

An insight into owning, restoring, servicing and flying
Britain's legendary World War II bomber

Jarrod Cotter and Paul Blackah

REMOVE BEFORE FLIGHT

Contents

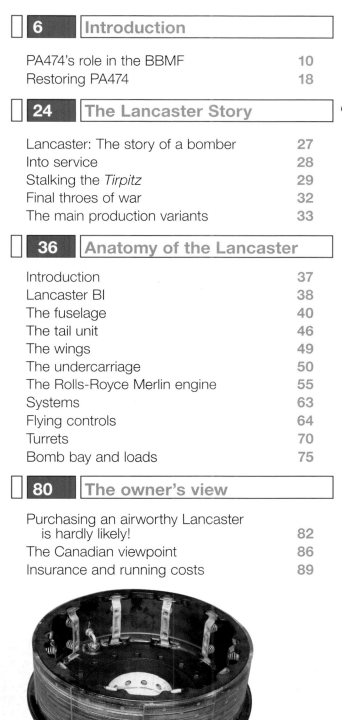

'I believe that the Lancaster
was the greatest single factor in
winning the war.'

Air Chief Marshal Sir Arthur Harris
December 1945

(Photo: Andrea Featherby)

Introduction

Over the years the Lancaster has won the hearts and souls of so many. From the Bomber Command aircrew that it brought home from dangerous operations over occupied enemy territory, to the airshow-goer who avidly gazes up as its unmistakable black shape flies gracefully across the peaceful skies that it helped secure.

That the Lancaster was born to wreak havoc on a distant enemy might be a disturbing thought to younger generations who, perhaps, see it as just a beautiful old aeroplane, 'harmless' even. But there is no mistaking that the 'Lanc' was in the thick of the fight during World War Two, playing a significant part in winning the freedom that we enjoy today.

Beautiful wartime study of a Lancaster almost head-on, high above the England it was protecting. *(RAF Museum)*

RIGHT The Lancaster's shape is unmistakable, and as PA474 travels to and from scheduled appearances each year it is seen by millions the length and breadth of the United Kingdom. *(Jarrod Cotter)*

OPPOSITE Night was the natural environment of the wartime Lancaster, so the rare sight of one in darkness nowadays always evokes a feeling of pre-'ops' tension, as though a crew were about to board for a sortie to some distant target, perhaps never to return. *(Chris Elcock/ Crown Copyright)*

If asked to name a Royal Air Force bomber from World War Two, most people in the UK would immediately answer 'Lancaster'. Avro's mighty four-engined workhorse gained its iconic status for numerous reasons. It was able to carry out its intended job efficiently, it was reliable, and it offered many advantages over its predecessors in Bomber Command. All of this combined to give Lancaster aircrews a better chance of making it home.

At the time, Lancaster aircrew would have considered it a 'tool of the trade', but in latter years they have been able to enjoy looking at it as the beautiful aeroplane that it is – thanks to the fact that it got them back from the severe hazards of 'ops' over occupied Europe. There is no doubt that the majority of the population of the United Kingdom admire and know of the Lancaster, as we are lucky enough to be living where one of only two airworthy examples in

The Battle of Britain Memorial Flight Lancaster: why PA474 was used as the main source of material for this book

The BBMF's Lancaster is without doubt the finest example of its type in the world. As well as being restored to authentic wartime configuration (with the exception of its dual controls), the fact that this bomber is still on the RAF's inventory, is based in 'Bomber County' from where many of its brethren set out on 'ops' to occupied Europe, and flies all over our island each summer providing millions of people with the chance to experience its evocative sight and sound, makes it a priceless national treasure.

As PA474 is kept in airworthy condition by the RAF, it must be operated and maintained in accordance with military regulations and procedures – which makes it the ideal principal source of material for this manual. While there is no question that the other extant Lancasters in museums all over the world are priceless and superbly maintained exhibits, the prospect of taking one of them to pieces for a book such as this is utterly beyond practicality. However, PA474 undergoes regular examination and maintenance to keep it in safe flying condition, which is why the majority of pictures in this book are of PA474 and its various component parts. Many of these photographs were especially taken to provide readers with a wonderful and unprecedented insight into how a Lancaster is maintained.

ABOVE RIGHT
PA474 wears the 550 Squadron BQ-B code to starboard, representing the unit with which *Phantom of the Ruhr* went on to become a 'Centurion', completing a total of 121 operations.
(Crown Copyright)

OPPOSITE Dedicated to the more than 55,000 Bomber Command personnel who never made it home to see the next morning's sunrise...
(Jarrod Cotter)

the world takes to the skies on a regular basis between April and September, courtesy of the Battle of Britain Memorial Flight based at RAF Coningsby in Lincolnshire. During World War Two Lincolnshire was known as 'Bomber County' on account of the number of bomber bases there.

Lancaster Mark I PA474 pays a 'living' tribute to the more than 55,000 Bomber Command personnel who didn't make it home, and to their comrades who survived the war but have had to live with their memories for the rest of their lives. Thus, each time PA474 arrives back in Lincolnshire – whether after a display, or after carrying out a flypast at a village fete or a high-profile State occasion – it symbolises all those lost souls finally making it home. May this continue for many years to come.

There is also a Lancaster maintained in airworthy condition in Canada, a country which

has very strong connections with the type. Not only did many Canadians serve with Bomber Command during World War Two, but Lancs were also built in Canada before being flown to England. After the war Lancasters were operated by the Royal Canadian Air Force in various roles too, so it is wholly appropriate that Mark X FM213 still graces the skies of Canada.

PA474's role in the BBMF

The BBMF was originally known as the Historic Aircraft Flight and was a direct result of the efforts of Wing Commander (later Group Captain) Peter Thompson DFC, then Station Commander at Biggin Hill, Kent. After gaining his wings in the summer of 1940, Peter flew Hurricanes during the Battle of Britain.

After the war the powers-that-be determined that Battle of Britain Day should be on 15 September, as in 1940 that date had marked the height of the aerial conflict. And so it was that in 1945 thousands gathered in London to watch masses of RAF fighters carry

out the first of what was to become an annual flypast over the capital. In the years immediately following World War Two it became traditional for a Hurricane and a Spitfire to lead the flypast.

With the passing of time, aircraft that were once the mainstay of RAF fighter operations decreased in numbers and gradually the jet age took over. The familiar and much-loved piston-engined types were rapidly withdrawn from frontline service.

By the mid-1950s Hurricane II LF363 was the only airworthy representative of its type with the RAF, and at that time was based at Biggin Hill. When the Spitfire was finally phased out of RAF service in 1957 the only three remaining airworthy examples were those being flown by the civilian-operated THUM (Temperature and Humidity) Flight at Woodvale, Lancs.

There was a strong belief among some in the RAF that the service's greatest Battle Honour (Battle of Britain) should continue to be commemorated in a fitting fashion – and the best way to do that was to keep these legendary fighters in the air. Wing Commander Thompson was an enthusiastic advocate of this notion and with LF363 already at Biggin, he had the basis for a grander plan. Peter gained the authority to form a commemorative unit, but no public funding for maintenance or fuel would be forthcoming and all manpower would have to be on a voluntary basis.

With their useful operational careers over, the three Spitfire PR XIXs of the THUM Flight – PM631, PS853 and PS915 – were allocated to the unit. They were scheduled to be delivered to Duxford, Cambridgeshire, on 12 June 1957, but PS915 proved unserviceable and PS853 ended up on its nose during take-off. Nevertheless, over the next few weeks all three arrived and awaited their RAF pilots.

From Duxford, a three-Spit formation eventually flew to Biggin on 11 July, piloted by legendary wartime ace Group Captain J.E. 'Johnnie' Johnson in PS853, Group Captain James Rankin in PM631 and Wing Commander Peter Thompson in PS915.

What was then known as the Historic Aircraft Flight (or HAF) was formed at Biggin Hill on 11 July 1957. However, while the concept had come to fruition there was a consensus among wartime pilots that it was not right to form a tribute flight to the Battle of Britain using a variant of the Spitfire that was not designed to fire guns. The solution came in the form of three Mark XVIs (TE330, TE476 and SL574), recently brought out of storage for a ground display at the 1957 Royal Tournament. The Senior Technical Officer at Biggin, Squadron Leader E.H. Sowden, recommended that priority be given to bringing these up to flying condition. This was partly because they were fighters, but also because spares were more readily available than for the PR XIXs.

Peter Thompson air-tested TE330 at Biggin early in September 1957. It performed faultlessly and was taxied across to the Station Flight hangar where it joined up with LF363. On 15 September, HAF carried out its first commemorative flight over Westminster Abbey for Battle of Britain Day, using LF363 and TE330. By that time the Flight had already lost one of its PR XIXs. PS915 had not been in the best of health when it arrived at Biggin Hill on 11 July, so it was retired from flying fairly promptly. Peter flew it to West Malling on 8 August, where it became a gate guardian. Two months later, on 10 December 1957, TE476 was successfully air-tested.

In February 1958 Peter was posted to the USA and promoted to Group Captain. He had always referred to the HAF as the 'BoB Flight' and on 21 February it was officially renamed as the Battle of Britain Flight. Work continued steadily and on the 23rd SL574 took to the skies. However, in the same month it was announced that Biggin was to close and the

Flight was informed it would move to North Weald in Essex by March 1958.

That April the BoB Flight lost a second PR XIX, as PS853 was allocated to West Raynham, Norfolk, where it was placed on display at the gate. In the following month it was dealt yet another blow, and one that must have been extremely frustrating – despite the existence of many non-airworthy Spitfires around the UK, the Flight's principal flyer, TE330, was taken away on 14 May to be prepared for presentation to the USAF Academy at Colorado Springs.

Things were going from bad to worse. In May 1958 North Weald closed, so that after a very brief stay there the BoB Flight was again in need of a new home. It moved to Martlesham Heath in Suffolk shortly afterwards, where it remained for three years.

It was here, during 1959, that the Flight lost its remaining Spitfire XVIs due to a series of accidents and reliability problems. On 28 May SL574 suffered a flying incident at Martlesham and was sent for repair to 71 Maintenance Unit

at Bicester, Oxfordshire, returning on 1 July. Then on 10 September TE476 had a wheels-up landing. As a result, the 'Top Brass' decreed that 20 September 1959 would be the last time the Flight's fighters, including Hurricane LF363, would participate in the Battle of Britain flypast over London. This decision was perhaps vindicated when SL574 suffered a complete engine failure during that very sortie over the capital and crash-landed on a cricket ground at Bromley.

In November 1961 the BoB Flight undertook another move, to Horsham St Faith in Norfolk. By this time it comprised just LF363 and PR XIX PM631, and this is how things would remain until 1964.

Continuing what could almost have been seen as a jinx, it transpired that Horsham in turn had been earmarked for closure, and on 1 April 1963 the Flight made its way to nearby Coltishall. After all these knock-backs, surely the BoB Flight was due some better luck?

Coltishall offered just such a chance and things began to improve significantly. PS853 was made serviceable again and put on charge of the Central Fighter Establishment on 31 October 1962. In April 1964 it was returned to the Flight. Then in September 1965 another Spitfire joined the ranks when Vickers-Armstrong parted with Mark VB AB910. This brought the Flight's inventory back up to four, and with the fleet and its popularity growing things were put on a more formal footing at Coltishall, resulting in the appointment of a team of full-time engineers.

Another significant acquisition occurred after filming for the 1969 classic movie *Battle of Britain* ended, when the Flight was presented with Spitfire IIA P7350 – the world's oldest airworthy example and a genuine combat veteran of the Battle of Britain.

Having popularly become known as the Battle of Britain Memorial Flight, the unit officially took this name on 1 June 1969.

Another major milestone came in March 1972, when Hurricane IIC PZ865 was presented to the BBMF after being refurbished by Hawker Siddeley. This aircraft had been the very last off the production line and hence carried the legend *The Last of the Many!* on its sides.

November 1973 saw the arrival of a new and significant wartime aircraft, which would widen the tribute paid by the BBMF to include Bomber Command as well as Fighter Command. On the 20th Lancaster I PA474 was officially transferred from Waddington, Lincs, where it had been refurbished and looked after by station personnel. It had been making a growing number of appearances around and about, and station resources were struggling to keep pace with the demand. The best option, it was realised, was to place PA474 under the care of the BBMF, which was better equipped with the necessary expertise and infrastructure to maintain it. However, the name of the BBMF remained unchanged and continued to reflect its dedication to the RAF's most famous Battle Honour.

Less than two years after the Lancaster arrived at Coltishall it was announced that the BBMF was moving to Coningsby in Lincolnshire, in order to free up its hangar space, and on 1 March 1976 the Flight began to ferry its aircraft to their new home. Though the BBMF had arrived at 'Colt' with just two wartime-era aircraft, it left with seven – including what was then the world's only airworthy Lancaster. Their arrival at Coningsby delighted the folk of Lincolnshire – often nicknamed 'Bomber County' – as they'd always had a

BELOW PA474 with a BBMF fighter escort of two Spitfires and a Hurricane. *(Crown Copyright)*

soft spot for their beloved Lancaster and had campaigned tirelessly to get it back.

The Flight's aircrew continues to comprise volunteers, who these days perform their primary duties working on front-line types such as the Eurofighter Typhoon and Boeing E-3D Sentry. The only exception is the BBMF's Officer Commanding, which is a full-time appointment owing to the additional demands of overseeing operations, administration and engineering.

For many years after its formation the Flight carried out relatively low-key operations, generally performing around 50 to 60 displays a year until the mid-1960s. Thereafter this figure gradually increased as the BBMF's popularity grew, and nowadays it's considered 'the norm' for between 700 and 800 individual appearances to be planned on the ops board. The BBMF has grown to become a major link between the RAF and the British public, and every year its aircraft are seen by around six million people. Since 1986 the Flight has even been made available to the public during weekdays – an amazing gesture of goodwill by the RAF. The BBMF Visitors' Centre features displays and a well-stocked shop, and for a nominal fee people can even go on a guided tour of the hangar.

As for the brave individuals who paid the ultimate price flying such aircraft to preserve our freedom, their sacrifice is honoured by the BBMF's motto… 'Lest We Forget'.

ABOVE Something which makes the BBMF even more of a priceless national asset is that it is not hidden away from the public. Each weekday visitors can pay a nominal fee to go on a guided tour of the Flight's hangar. In the winter they get to see the aircraft undergoing servicing such as this, while in the summer they may be lucky enough for their visit to coincide with aircraft starting up for a sortie.
(Jarrod Cotter)

LEFT For the Flight's 50th anniversary, PA474 led all seven BBMF fighters for one, possibly never-to-be-repeated flypast at Duxford on 5 May 2007.
(Jarrod Cotter)

Restoring PA474

PA474 was built as a BI by Vickers-Armstrong at Hawarden, North Wales, in 1945. Initially it was earmarked for 'Tiger Force' operations and, consequently, service in the Far East, so it was manufactured to FE standards. However, the war with Japan ended before it could take part in hostilities. Instead it went into storage at 38 Maintenance Unit, Llandow, South Wales, on 18 August 1945. It was next moved to 32 Maintenance Unit at St Athan, also in South Wales, on 26 November 1946.

After this period in storage PA474 was converted to PR1 configuration by Armstrong Whitworth, with work beginning on 28 June 1947. The conversion included the removal of the Lancaster's turrets. The former bomber was ferried back to Llandow on 11 August and temporarily placed back into storage.

On 23 September 1948, PA474 at last entered service with the RAF when it was assigned to 'B' Flight of No 82 Squadron for photographic reconnaissance duties in East

and South Africa. After joining the squadron at Benson, Oxfordshire, it was given the identification letter 'M', and spent the next four years carrying out survey work. This saw PA474 taken on many detachments to small airfields with relatively primitive facilities before it finally returned to Benson on 18 February 1952 to await a fairly uncertain future.

The bomber's long-term fate became even more doubtful when, from 26 May 1952, it was loaned to Flight Refuelling Ltd at Tarrant Rushton, Dorset, with the intention of converting it into a pilotless drone. Much design work followed while PA474 languished somewhat forgotten at Tarrant Rushton. However, before the proposed work began the Air Ministry decided to use an Avro Lincoln instead.

So on 7 March 1954 PA474 was transferred to the College of Aeronautics at Cranfield, Bedfordshire, where it was to be used for trials with several experimental aerofoil sections. This new career effectively saved an airworthy Lancaster for the nation. The trial wing sections were mounted vertically on the upper rear

BELOW PA474 in service with the College of Aeronautics while on laminar wing flow tests. *(College of Aeronautics)*

ABOVE PA474 minus
propellers, parked
outside Hangar 4 at
Waddington on 9 June
1971. *(Crown Copyright)*

LEFT A happy scene
at Waddington on 7
November 1967 after
PA474's first post-
restoration test flight.
(Crown Copyright)

fuselage of the aircraft, which at the time was still wearing its No 82 Squadron badges and individual 'M' code.

PA474 was employed in this role until 1964, by which time the College of Aeronautics had completed the conversion of Lincoln B2 G-36-3 (the former RF342) to replace it. During October 1963 the RAF had talked to the College about taking PA474 back with a view to putting it on display in the then planned RAF Museum, and on 22 April 1964 it was ferried to 15 Maintenance Unit at Wroughton, Wiltshire, and placed into storage. The first steps towards PA474 becoming a permanent flying memorial to Bomber Command had successfully been taken.

The aircraft was adopted by the Air Historical Branch with the intention of it being included in the new museum. It was soon painted in more fitting wartime camouflage, though without any squadron markings, and on 25 September 1964 was moved to RAF Henlow, Bedfordshire, to be prepared for the RAF Museum.

The first unit to be equipped with Lancasters had been No 44 (Rhodesia) Squadron, and in 1965 Wing Commander M.A. D'Arcy, the Commanding Officer of No 44 (by then flying Avro Vulcans from RAF Waddington in Lincolnshire) put in a request to the Ministry of Defence that PA474 be transferred to his squadron's care. Approval being eventually obtained, a party of ground crew left for Henlow on 12 May 1965.

On close inspection PA474 appeared to be airworthy, so a further request was sent to the MoD asking that it be flown to Waddington. After due consideration this request too was granted, and on 26 July a team of experienced technicians from Waddington started a 'recovery servicing'. This included undercarriage retraction tests, complete engine runs, compass swing, flying control checks, electrical and instrument system checks and wheel brake

BELOW PA474 on 6 November 1974, partway through a Major overhaul at Kemble. *(Crown Copyright)*

checks. Despite having stood out in the open for 12 months, the only servicing required on the Merlins was the clearing out of birds' nests from the cowlings, spark plug cleaning, and fuel and oil checks! The engines started easily.

After PA474 was declared fully serviceable the aircrew arrived on 18 August for what was supposed to be its last flight, to Waddington. At 10:30am the crew climbed aboard and the pre-flight checks were carried out.

One by one the Merlins burst into life, chocks were drawn away, and PA474 taxied across the rough grass field to the take-off point. A fair-sized crowd had gathered to watch the proceedings, and they were rewarded by the evocative sight of the Lancaster slowly gathering speed and rising off the ground. Its departure caused much surprise around Henlow, where it had been regarded as a mere museum relic, and never expected to fly, so there was hardly a door or window on the camp from which heads didn't appear when

LEFT A major milestone in PA474's restoration to authentic wartime configuration was the fitting of a mid-upper turret, seen here being lowered into position during 1976 under the guidance of Pete 'Gerbs' Jeffery and Engineering Officer Flight Lieutenant Terry Lees. *(Crown Copyright)*

BELOW RAF engineers hard at work about to remove the nose section of PA474 at Abingdon, circa 1983. *(Crown Copyright)*

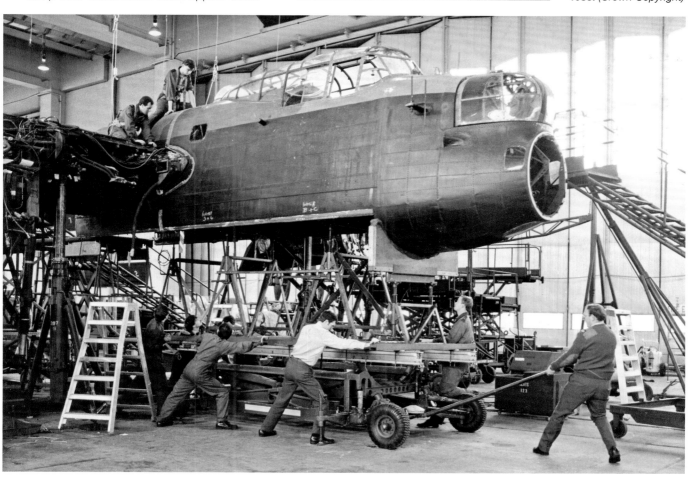

ABOVE Again seen
at Abingdon in 1983,
the Lancaster's rear
fuselage has been
separated from the
centre section. Note
that at the time it
was wearing the
AJ-G markings of
Wing Commander
Guy Gibson's ED932
from the famous
'Dam Busters' raid.
(Crown Copyright)

PA474 flew over! It made for Waddington in the company of a Varsity that had been provided for the press and television crews.

At Lincoln the Lancaster made several runs past the Cathedral so that the photographers could film it with that landmark in the background. The Varsity then flew on to land at Waddington first so that the photographers could position themselves to film the Lancaster's arrival. Meanwhile, it made two low, fast runs down Scampton's main runway before landing at Waddington at 1:30pm.

After being put into storage in one of Waddington's hangars it was decided to repaint the Lancaster in the markings of Squadron Leader J.D. Nettleton's KM-B, in which he earned his Victoria Cross whilst carrying out the famous low-level daylight raid on the MAN factory at Augsburg on 17 April 1942. The markings were those of No 44 Squadron Lancaster I R5508.

A restoration programme then began that would continue for many years. By 1966 work was progressing well and both the front and rear turrets were in place. However, the Lancaster was initially intended to be only a static exhibit, as its return to the air would require overcoming many difficulties. Instead it stood on display outside the Officers' Mess – until Group Captain Arthur Griffiths AFC, Waddington's Station Commander since April 1967, saw it and asked why it wasn't being flown. Group Captain Griffiths was a true flyer who simply loved aeroplanes, and he just couldn't bear to see PA474 looking forlorn and unwanted. He decided to attempt making the Lancaster airworthy again, and to get the necessary permission to fly it.

The project was supported by HQ 1 Group, but foundered initially with the MoD from whom financial approval was slow in coming. What finally carried the day was the forthcoming 50th anniversary of Waddington in November 1967. The celebrations were to culminate with a guest night in the Officers' Mess, to which Chief of Defence Staff MRAF Sir Charles Elworthy (a former OC Waddington) and many other distinguished guests had been invited.

The plan was to get the Lancaster airborne before this date.

On 6 November permission for one air test finally arrived. After an hour's circuit work in a borrowed Hastings on 7 November to refamiliarise himself with such peculiarities as propellers, flaps and tailwheels, Waddington's Station Commander went to the Lancaster, started up the 'four lovely Merlins' and taxied out. He pushed the throttles open and away they went, with no problems at all. The aircraft flew beautifully and was obviously delighted to be back in the air after so many years.

The flight was well received in higher headquarters and the Lancaster was subsequently allowed to fly on further occasional test flights. Nevertheless, there were still to be difficulties from time to time. Propeller oil leaks were a problem until some appropriate seals were obtained from Hong Kong. Feathering motors appeared unobtainable until MoD Harrogate bought a couple from a local scrap dealer. On one occasion, a double plug failure caused such vibration that the Lancaster's No 4 engine had to be shut down, necessitating the pilot's first three-piston-engined landing for 20 years! But by and large PA474 continued to fly beautifully, and the only real problem lay in gaining financial authority to fly it regularly. Gradually, as the aircraft continued to give little trouble and gained in popularity, opposition decreased and the Waddington Lancaster was invited increasingly to air shows throughout England, where it was always the star attraction.

Restoration work to bring the bomber up to the desired condition to accurately represent a wartime Lanc went on. PA474 joined the BBMF in November 1973 and in 1975 it was adopted by the City of Lincoln, the name and coat of arms of which it still proudly wears more than 30 years later. When the BBMF moved to its current home at RAF Coningsby, Lincolnshire, in 1976 restoration work was still going on, and a mid-upper turret that had been discovered in Argentina, of all places, was finally fitted the same year. Even today work continues to get PA474 into an even more authentic wartime condition, the latest items being considered for addition being flame dampers over the exhaust shrouds.

The only Lancaster to be re-sparred

On 25 September 1995, having completed the year's display season, PA474 set off from Coningsby and flew to St Athan to undergo a major wing re-spar programme. This had never been done before; the lifespan of a wartime Lanc was expected to be relatively short, so there had been no need to consider that one might ever need replacement wing spars.

A fatigue meter had been fitted on board PA474. By the end of the 1983 flying season readings showed that the bomber had clocked up 3,060 hours, leaving 1,340 hours or about 13 years remaining, based on its usage at that time. In 1984 British Aerospace (BAe) determined the fatigue index to be 70.7, where an index of 100 indicates no fatigue life remaining. A decision that the spar booms would eventually need to be replaced was made in 1990, and BAe was tasked to define the repair.

The intention of the repair design was to replicate as much of the historic concept of the Lancaster as possible. This included the use of a unique method of attaching the skins to the boom on the outer wings, known as plug riveting. However, the repair could not in any way compromise modern-day design practices and fatigue enhancement measures.

The new booms were to be manufactured from extrusions surplus to the re-sparring programme of the RAF's Avro Shackletons. They were to be made without drilling any holes so that the drilling pattern could be copied from the existing booms. In addition the repairs were required to include new webs and fasteners and new shackles.

A decision was made to keep PA474 flying for as long as sufficient fatigue life remained available on the original spars, which had been calculated to expire in 1996. Flying restrictions were imposed to avoid any heavy manoeuvres, and fatigue meter readings were regularly sent to BAe for analysis.

As the booms were the critical components they were wisely manufactured well in advance of the repair date and consequently completed in December 1993. Later it was agreed that the repair work would be performed by BAe at Chadderton, near Manchester. In July 1995 BAe formally accepted the contract to carry out the re-sparring.

After its arrival at St Athan in 1995 PA474 was separated into its component parts and prepared for transportation. Various sections arrived at BAe in November and were placed in purpose-built holding fixtures to support them during the work. Around 5,000 production hours were spent on the aircraft by both military and civilian engineers, who often worked from 07:30 until 20:00, before completed sections were ready to be sent back to St Athan during early February 1996.

The bomber was reassembled at St Athan, and its first flight test was carried out on 13 May. Two days later PA474 returned to Coningsby with its new spar in place – and with its annual flying time carefully restricted this will enable it to fly for many years to come.

A staggering 500,000 manufacturing processes were involved in building the Lancaster, which was made up of 55,000 separate parts.

Chapter One

The Lancaster Story

The origins of the Lancaster can be traced back to 1936 when the RAF was looking to re-equip with up-to-date monoplane bombers. Air Ministry Specification P.13/36 for a so-called 'medium bomber' formed the basis of the design for Avro's twin-engine Manchester.

However, the genesis of the Lancaster lay in the failure of the Manchester's twin Rolls-Royce Vulture engines. Four Merlins were married to the Manchester airframe and the resulting aircraft was called the Manchester III – later renamed the Lancaster.

LEFT Lancaster I R5689 VN-N of No 50 Squadron. On the night of 18 September 1942 this aircraft took off from Swinderby, Lincolnshire, on a 'Gardening' sortie to an undisclosed area. It was badly hit and attempted to return, but crash-landed some miles south of its base at Thurlby, Lincolnshire, when both port engines failed as the crew prepared for landing. *(RAF Museum)*

Lancaster:
The story of a bomber

One of the most revolutionary departures from previous aircraft design practice was the proposed increase in wing loading. This would allow a heavier type of aircraft to be operated from airfields that would most likely have grass or even sandy surfaces. Up to that time the normal wing loadings were in the region of 20lb/ft sq, but the Avro Manchester design called for double that. This caused numerous headaches for the design team, as the engine loading could not be reduced to compensate for the effect of the higher wing loading on the take-off run, and the rate of climb once off the ground, though a degree of compensation was offered by the constant speed variable pitch propeller which was being developed.

After many trials and tribulations with the design, A.V. Roe & Company Limited first flew the Avro 679 Manchester twin-engined medium bomber on 25 July 1939 from Ringway, Manchester. The Manchester was the brainchild of Avro's chief designer Roy Chadwick, and was powered by a pair of Rolls-Royce Vulture engines. By the end of January 1940 some 1,200 Manchesters had been ordered, but only 200 were delivered due to reliability problems with the Vulture and the Manchester's performance. For example, its 'comfortable' operating altitude was between 10,000ft and 15,000ft, leaving it vulnerable to flak which was becoming more and more of a danger. However, one feature of the Manchester which was an indisputable success was its bomb bay.

With the Rolls-Royce Merlin proving to be an excellent engine, and with more powerful marks being planned, it was decided not to waste any time in trying to improve the Vulture. This cancellation left Avro with a superb airframe in need of a reliable power plant.

In February 1940 discussions had taken place regarding a proposed Manchester III powered by four Merlins. There was some initial reluctance about this, as at the time Merlins were desperately needed for Hurricanes and Spitfires. However, in July 1940 there was a change of heart and the Air Ministry informed Avro of their wish that the development of the four-engined Manchester should go ahead.

The Avro 683 was to have the minimum of changes from the production Manchester, which had already received approval for an increase of its wingspan from 80ft to 90ft. The new design had a proposed wingspan of 100ft, though the Lancaster eventually had a 102ft wingspan. To meet the demanding schedules, it was strongly felt that the retention of the Avro 679 centre section would be crucial.

After a number of setbacks Avro got the approval to produce two prototypes by July 1941. The first of these, BT308, was rolled out for engine runs on 28 December 1940. By 4 January 1941 the four-engined Avro 683 was cleared to fly from Woodford. However, due to poor weather – low cloud, drizzle and fog – it was temporarily grounded.

By 9 January the weather had improved sufficiently for BT308 to take to the skies – and the Lancaster legend was born! While the aircraft was still widely known as the Manchester III it was annotated as a 'Lancaster' on its Air Ministry Form 1187 Design Certificate for Flight Trials.

BT308 initially featured the triple fin design of the Manchester. However, following early handling trials it was suggested that the aircraft be fitted with larger twin fins and the central fin be removed. It was first flown in this form on 21 February 1941, and such was the improvement that on its second test flight BT308 was flown with both port engines shut down – proving that the larger rudders could keep the bomber flying straight.

The second prototype, DG595, carried out its maiden flight on 13 May 1941, and it quickly received authorisation to go for service trials. Though there were delays, Roy Chadwick used the time wisely and set about improving a number of areas he had already identified as needing attention, as well as initiating a complete review of the aircraft and its systems. With Manchester production now ceased, the Lancaster was approved and the balance of orders was changed to the new four-engined bomber. The first production machine, L7527, flew on 31 October 1941.

L7527 differed from the prototypes in that it had four 1,280hp Merlin XXs rather than 1,145hp Merlin Xs. The aircraft's performance

ABOVE A staggering 500,000 manufacturing processes were involved in building a Lancaster, which was made up of some 55,000 separate parts – even when you count engines and turrets as one item and exclude all the rivets, nuts and bolts! *(RAF Museum)*

OPPOSITE As the light fades a formation of Lancasters sets out for occupied Europe. A few hours later they were probably avoiding flak in the night skies over a heavily defended target. *(RAF Museum)*

was simply outstanding; large-scale production soon began at several factories and plans were put in place to get the Lancaster built in Canada too.

The first RAF unit to receive the Lancaster was 44 (Rhodesia) Squadron at Waddington, Lincolnshire. On Christmas Eve 1941 the squadron took delivery of three examples of the type.

Into service

It was not until 3 March 1942 that the Lancaster entered operational service, when four aircraft from No 44 Squadron set off for Heligoland Bight in the North Sea at the mouth of the River Elbe, on a mine-laying sortie. They took off from Waddington at 18:15 and all returned safely around five hours later.

The first night bombing operation with Lancasters took place a week later on 10/11 March, when two 44 Squadron Lancs took part in a raid on Essen. Each of them carried 5,000lb of incendiaries and they joined a force of 126 bombers which included Handley Page Hampdens, Manchesters, Short Stirlings and

Vickers Wellingtons. Lancasters were certainly well received by their crews, and they quickly settled into squadron service, proving themselves to be sound and reliable workhorses.

Many raids by Lancasters would go on to make headline news, the first of these being the daylight operation by 44 and 97 Squadrons to bomb the MAN Diesel factory at Augsburg in southern Germany on 17 April 1942. Squadron Leader J.D. Nettleton vc of 44 Squadron led the 12-aircraft op, for which he became the first of ten Lancaster aircrew to be awarded the Victoria Cross for their exploits.

Lancasters were in service in time to participate in the first 'Thousand Bomber' raid on the night of 30/31 May 1942, codenamed Operation Millennium. Out of a total of 1,047 aircraft that were despatched to Cologne, 868 reached the primary target.

On the clear moonlit night of 16/17 May 1943 the newly formed 617 Squadron successfully carried out what became the most famous single operation in the history of aerial warfare. No 617 Squadron, commanded by Wing Commander Guy Gibson, set out from Scampton in Lincolnshire to breach key dams in the industrial heartland of Germany. For the sortie the squadron used a special weapon (codenamed 'Upkeep' and actually termed a mine, but more commonly referred to as the 'bouncing bomb') that had been designed by the famous and highly respected aviation designer Sir Barnes Wallis.

The Lancasters used for the raid were BIII (Specials), modified to be able to carry one mine each in a specially designed calliper device that could rotate it at the 500rpm required for it to work successfully. Furthermore, the bomb would need to be dropped from just 60ft, at night, and at a specified speed and exact distance from the dams. To compound things further, the crews had just seven weeks to train for the precision attack as it had to take place within a narrow timeframe.

Nineteen aircraft set out, with sixteen reaching their targets. Operation Chastise was carried out successfully, with the Möhne and Eder Dams both being breached and the Sorpe damaged. Of the sixteen Lancs that reached their targets eight were lost, and only three of their 56 crew members survived to become prisoners of war.

It was for this famous operation that Guy Gibson was awarded the VC, with a total of 34 decorations being awarded for aircrew who participated in Chastise. The post-raid publicity was massive, and proved to be a tremendous PR boost for the RAF.

Stalking the *Tirpitz*

Another very famous achievement using Lancasters came as a result of the three operations mounted to sink the mighty German battleship *Tirpitz*. Along with 617 Squadron, as the war progressed 9 Squadron also came to specialise in dropping large bombs, in particular the 12,000lb 'Tallboy', on strategic targets – and the ops aimed at destroying the *Tirpitz* are a further good example of the Lanc's operational versatility.

In January 1942 Prime Minister Winston Churchill put out a document to the Chiefs of Staff stating that no other sea target was comparable to the *Tirpitz* – the entire worldwide naval situation would be altered if it could be destroyed, or even crippled. Although a

number of attempts by various units were made to sink the vessel, it remained serviceable. Consequently 9 and 617 Squadrons were tasked to bomb the *Tirpitz* during September 1944 in Operation Paravane. Armed with 'Tallboys', they were to fly to Yagodnik in the Soviet Union so that they would be within range of the German battleship.

A number of aircraft from both squadrons were lost en route to Yagodnik, but the remaining force set out from the Russian airfield on 15 September to bomb the *Tirpitz* in its Norwegian hiding place at Kaafjord. The crucial element of surprise was lost when a German ground unit gave prior notice of the bomber force's direction, and a smoke screen was set up over the ship. Attempts were nevertheless made to bomb the *Tirpitz*, but many of the post-flight reports state that the target was obscured by smoke that made the results difficult to determine.

Later it was discovered that the *Tirpitz* had indeed been hit by one 'Tallboy' that had gone through the forward deck and emerged below the waterline on the starboard side before exploding, while a second near miss had caused further damage. These bombs are thought to have been dropped by 9 Squadron's Flight Lieutenant J.D. Melrose and 617 Squadron's Wing Commander J.B. Tait DSO* DFC***. The attack had, however, rendered *Tirpitz* unfit to go to sea.

The damage having been patched up by mid-October, the huge vessel was then moved to the port of Tromsø, around 200 miles south of its previous location. This new berth potentially put the battleship within range of RAF bases in north-east Scotland, including Lossiemouth.

In order to carry out attacks, however, the Lancasters would have to be heavily modified and fitted with the more powerful Merlin 24s

BELOW While most stories obviously relate to the aircrew, they in turn all testify that the contribution of their ground crews was critical. *(RAF Museum)*

– but the only ones available were already fitted to other Lancasters scattered throughout 5 Group. A frantic search located all the Merlin 24s and these were then exchanged with the engines fitted to the 'Tallboy' aircraft. Other modifications included removing the mid-upper turrets, pilot's armour, guns and ammunition from the front turrets, and gas bottles, plus reducing the amount of ammunition carried in the rear turret. Extra fuel tanks were then fitted to give the aircraft sufficient range.

More than 120 engines were exchanged over a three-day period – this and all the other modifications had to be carried out on top of routine maintenance and repairs, thus confirming 9 Squadron's unofficial motto: 'There's always bloody something'!

A combined force of 40 Lancasters (20 from 9 Squadron, 19 from 617 Squadron, and PD329 from No 463 Squadron on 'special photographic duties') left their bases for Scotland on 28 October, and the following day set off for Tromsø on Operation Obviate. Heavily laden with extra fuel and weighty 'Tallboys', the aircraft took off at +18 boost rather than the normal +14.

On approach to the target area an unexpected weather front caused conditions to rapidly deteriorate and bombing was made difficult as the target quickly became obscured by cloud. Some aircraft dropped bombs by targeting the gun flashes they could glimpse through the cloud, but as the force turned for home the crews knew that the *Tirpitz* was still afloat. It was later reported that had the attack happened just half an hour earlier conditions would have been perfect.

A third attempt by 9 and 617 Squadrons to bomb the *Tirpitz* was initiated during November. At 03:00 on 12 November 1944 the first of the Lancasters set off from Scotland on Operation Catechism. This time they had perfect weather

BELOW Last RAF sortie by a Lancaster, as MR3 RF325 carries out a flypast at St Mawgan in Cornwall on 15 October 1956. *(MoD/Crown Copyright)*

conditions all the way to the target, with the clear sky offering excellent visibility.

As the Lancasters neared the battleship they were greeted by flak, but with their armament depleted to save weight there was a more serious risk that the Lancasters might become very easy prey to the *Tirpitz*'s fighter cover. Indeed, ground troops reported the bomber force to be heading towards the vessel and its Captain ordered that the fighters be scrambled, knowing they could be overhead in ten minutes. However, the 18 Focke-Wulf Fw190s that got aloft set off in the wrong direction – they had apparently not been informed of the battleship's change of anchorage!

Everything was at last in favour of a successful attack. The 'Tallboys' rained down on the *Tirpitz* and after a number of direct hits and near misses the battleship rolled over to port and lay on its side. Huge clouds of black smoke rose into the gin-clear sky. The Lancaster crews' determination to finish off this significant threat had finally paid off.

Final throes of war

After the 'Tallboy' came the 22,000lb 'Grand Slam', sometimes called the 'Earthquake bomb'. To carry this the Lancaster had to again be modified, with the huge bombs being slung externally in a doorless bomb bay. The first use of the 'Grand Slam' came on 14 March 1945, when the Bielefeld Viaduct in northern Germany was attacked. The Lancasters capable of carrying 'Grand Slams' became known as 'Clapper' aircraft by their crews, because after releasing their heavy payloads the aircraft 'went like the clappers'!

Another high-profile mission which came late in the war was the daylight raid to bomb Hitler's 'Eagle's Nest' retreat at Berchtesgaden. This op to the Bavarian Alps was carried out on 25 April 1945, and though Hitler was not in residence at the time it was still considered a success. The same day saw Lancasters take off for the last raid by the type, a night op against an oil target at Tonsberg in Norway on 25/26 April.

Lancasters not only made a vital and hugely significant contribution to Bomber Command's night offensive, but they also helped to turn the tide in the major land battles of 1944 by bombing the German army in the field and flying tactical sorties aimed at precision targets. During the war Lancasters carried out around 156,000 sorties and dropped 608,612 tons of bombs.

Before the German surrender Lancasters were heavily involved in Operation Manna, which saw them supplying much-needed food to starving Dutch people. These sorties were potentially hazardous as large areas of the country were still under German control – though with the war's end in sight a truce was negotiated and the Lancs were allowed to carry out their vital aid relief largely unhindered. Some 6,684 tons of food were dropped during 2,835 sorties.

Following the end of hostilities in Europe Lancasters were put to use in another passive role, being used to repatriate liberated Allied prisoners of war back to England, this task being codenamed Operation Exodus.

After the war a number of Bomber Command units continued to be equipped with the Lancaster until the type was replaced by the Avro Lincoln. The last bomber unit to operate Lancs, 49 Squadron, converted to Lincolns in March 1950.

With the departure of the lend-lease Consolidated Liberators after the war the Lancaster became the principal land-based maritime reconnaissance aircraft used by Coastal Command. The last example of the type to be operated in service by the RAF was MR3 RF325, which was used by the School of Maritime Reconnaissance at RAF St Mawgan in Cornwall and was retired on 15 October 1956. Sadly, after a farewell ceremony it was flown away to Wroughton, Wiltshire, to be scrapped.

The Lancaster also formally served with some other countries post-war. It served on with the Royal Canadian Air Force for some 20 years, operating in a variety of roles including air-sea rescue. The air forces of Argentina and Egypt also used the Lanc, as did the French Navy. The Soviet Air Force assembled two examples from those that had force-landed in Russia during the first of the *Tirpitz* raids, the Royal Australian Air Force had two Lancs on its books, and the Swedish Air Force used a Lancaster as an engine test bed. Many Lancasters were also used in experimental and development trials, and some were put onto the civilian registers of Britain and Canada.

The main production variants

BI – Powered by four Rolls-Royce Merlin XXs, 22s or 24s. Most numerous mark built, followed closely by the Mark III. The Mark I and Mark III differed only in respect of the power plants and associated services and controls. The first production example carried out its maiden flight on 31 October 1941.

BI (Special) – Modified to carry loads in excess of 12,000lb, notably the huge 22,000lb 'Grand Slam' bomb. In order to carry such a large and heavy weapon the BI (Special) had to have it slung externally in a doorless 'cutaway' bomb bay area, and had to be fitted with the more powerful Merlin 24s. The first use of the 'Grand Slam' came on 14 March 1945, when the Bielefeld Viaduct was attacked. The 'Grand Slam' gained the name 'Earthquake bomb' due to the effect of such a large explosion. The extra

designation 'Special' was applied to aircraft modified in various ways for specific weapons.

BII – Built by Armstrong Whitworth and powered by Bristol Hercules VI radial engines, and later the Hercules XVI. This was the first attempt to overcome the problem of Rolls-Royce Merlins not being built fast enough to satisfy an ever-

TOP Lancaster I seen in March 1944 with H2S radar dome visible underneath the rear fuselage. *(A&AEE)*

ABOVE Lancaster II fitted with Bristol Hercules radial engines. *(Air Ministry)*

LEFT Fitted with American-built Merlin 28s, this is Lancaster III prototype W4114, photographed in September 1942. *(Air Ministry)*

RIGHT ED817 was a BIII (Special) equipped with gear to hold and rotate an 'Upkeep' mine, more familiarly known as a 'bouncing bomb', for the famous 617 Squadron 'Dam Busters' raid of 16/17 May 1943. *(A&AEE)*

RIGHT The final evolution of the Lancaster's bomb-carrying capability was the BI (Special), which was modified to carry the huge 22,000lb 'Grand Slam' externally. *(Air Ministry)*

BELOW One of the few Lancaster VIs, which were fitted with powerful Merlin 85s or 87s and with modified air intakes. *(Ministry of Aircraft Production)*

increasing demand. When powered by the Hercules XVI the Mark II could attain a similar speed to its Merlin-powered brethren, though when fully bombed up it could not reach the same height and had a higher fuel consumption. Of the 300 Mark IIs built, some served with 61 Squadron but most were on the strength of 115 Squadron, which operated them from March 1943 until April 1944.

BIII – Fitted with Packard-built Merlin 28, 38 or 224 engines. After attempting to power Lancasters using Bristol Hercules engines, American-built Merlins were adopted as a better way of keeping pace with the increasing demand for this reliable and powerful engine. The Packard-built Merlin 28 delivered 1,300hp and differed from British-built examples in a

number of ways including carburetion. The Merlin 38 (equivalent to the British Mark 22) provided 1,390hp, and the Packard Merlin 224 was the equivalent to the powerful British Mark 24. The Packard engines were first trialled on Lancasters in August 1942 using Mark Is R5849 and W4114 – the latter gaining the status of the prototype Mark III. The Mark I and III had almost identical performance, but the new designation arose because there were different servicing procedures. It is reported that the Mark III gave better fuel consumption.

BIII (Special) – Otherwise called Type 464 Provisioning, 23 Lancasters were specially modified to carry 9,250lb 'Upkeep' mines for the 617 Squadron dams raid of 16/17 May 1943. The weapon was carried in a specially

LEFT Lancaster VII
NX612 in white 'Tiger
Force' paint scheme.
(Ministry of Supply)

LEFT Lancaster VII
NX612 in white 'Tiger
Force' paint scheme.
(Ministry of Supply)

MIDDLE The
RCAF used the five
Lancasters converted
to 10Ns as navigation
trainers, four of which
gained names. This is
FM211 *Zenith*.
(Nat Def Photograph)

BELOW Nine Lancaster
Xs were modified to
10P standard for photo
reconnaissance and
mapping work.
(Nat Def Photograph)

designed structure that could rotate it at the
500rpm required for it to work successfully.

Mark VII – Built by Austin, some of them
to 'FE' (Far East) standard for use with the
proposed Tiger Force for potential operations
in tropical conditions. Included an electrically-
powered Martin mid-upper turret. A batch of
150 BVIIs earmarked for Tiger Force were
fitted with 1,640hp Merlin 24s, which were
particularly suitable for use in the climate of
its intended theatre of operations. However,
the earlier than anticipated surrender of Japan
meant that these bombers saw no action in the
Far East.

Mark X – Canadian-built aircraft manufactured
by Victory Aircraft at Malton, Ontario. Fitted
with Packard-built Merlins. Later examples had
Martin 250/CE Type 23A electric mid-upper
turrets fitted further forward on the fuselage
and equipped with two 0.5in machine guns
rather than Browning 0.303s. All sections were
fully interchangeable with British-built parts in
case of battle damage.

Some other variants
PRI – For photo reconnaissance. Conversion
work included the removal of the turrets.
ASRIII – For air-sea rescue duties. Modified to
carry the Cunliff-Owen Airborne Lifeboat IIA.
MRIII/GRIII – Converted for maritime
reconnaissance, to replace Coastal
Command's Consolidated Liberators returned
to the USA when the Lend-Lease agreement
ended.
Mark VI – In order to increase the performance
of the Mark III, a small number of Lancasters
were fitted with higher-powered Merlin 85s or
87s and designated Mark VIs.

RCAF Post-war Lancaster Mark 10 conversion roles

Mark	Duties	Numbers/notes
10AR	Arctic reconnaissance	KB839/882/976
10BR	Bomber reconnaissance	Four 10ARs initially modified to 10BR (Interim) standard, then nine BXs converted to 10BR
10DC	Drone carrying	KB848/851
10MR/MP	Maritime reconnaissance/ patrol	Approximately 70
10N	Navigation trainer	FM206/208/211/KB826/986
10O	Avro Orenda engine test bed	FM209
10P	Photographic reconnaissance	FM120/122/199/207/212/214-218/KB729
10S	Standard post-war bomber	KB944/781/801/854
10SR	Air-Sea Rescue	FM148/222/KB907/961
10U	Standard bomber	Unmodified

Because of its size, the Lancaster fuselage is divided into five sections. When bolted together they form the main fuselage.

(Paul Blackah/Crown Copyright)

Chapter Two

Anatomy of the Lancaster

Although the BBMF and Canadian Warplane Heritage operate the only two flying Lancasters in the world there are still many ground-based examples to be seen, some of which are able to run their engines and taxi. Despite being constructed under wartime conditions, these aircraft are a true representation of the 'built to last' mentality. The BBMF is fortunate to have many of the original manuals and drawings, which enable them to maintain their aircraft to a high standard. The following sections should provide readers with a better understanding of the design, maintenance and servicing arrangements of this well-loved aircraft.

Lancaster BI

(Drawing: J.H. Clark, courtesy Aeroplane Monthly*/www.aeroplanemonthly.com)*

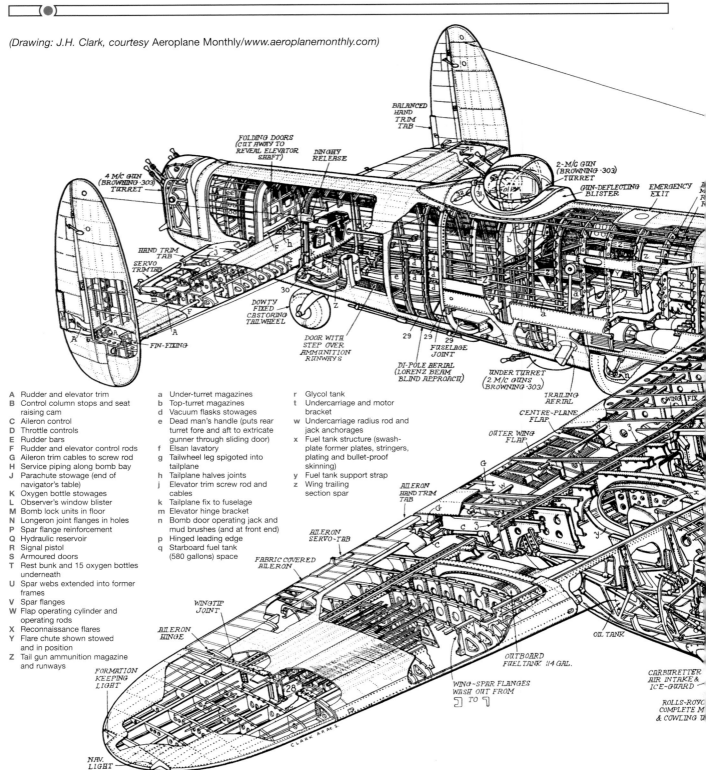

A Rudder and elevator trim
B Control column stops and seat raising cam
C Aileron control
D Throttle controls
E Rudder bars
F Rudder and elevator control rods
G Aileron trim cables to screw rod
H Service piping along bomb bay
J Parachute stowage (end of navigator's table)
K Oxygen bottle stowages
L Observer's window blister
M Bomb lock units in floor
N Longeron joint flanges in holes
P Spar flange reinforcement
Q Hydraulic reservoir
R Signal pistol
S Armoured doors
T Rest bunk and 15 oxygen bottles underneath
U Spar webs extended into former frames
V Spar flanges
W Flap operating cylinder and operating rods
X Reconnaissance flares
Y Flare chute shown stowed and in position
Z Tail gun ammunition magazine and runways

a Under-turret magazines
b Top-turret magazines
d Vacuum flasks stowages
e Dead man's handle (puts rear turret fore and aft to extricate gunner through sliding door)
f Elsan lavatory
g Tailwheel leg spigoted into tailplane
h Tailplane halves joints
j Elevator trim screw rod and cables
k Tailplane fix to fuselage
m Elevator hinge bracket
n Bomb door operating jack and mud brushes (and at front end)
p Hinged leading edge
q Starboard fuel tank (580 gallons) space

r Glycol tank
t Undercarriage and motor bracket
w Undercarriage radius rod and jack anchorages
x Fuel tank structure (swash-plate former plates, stringers, plating and bullet-proof skinning)
y Fuel tank support strap
z Wing trailing section spar

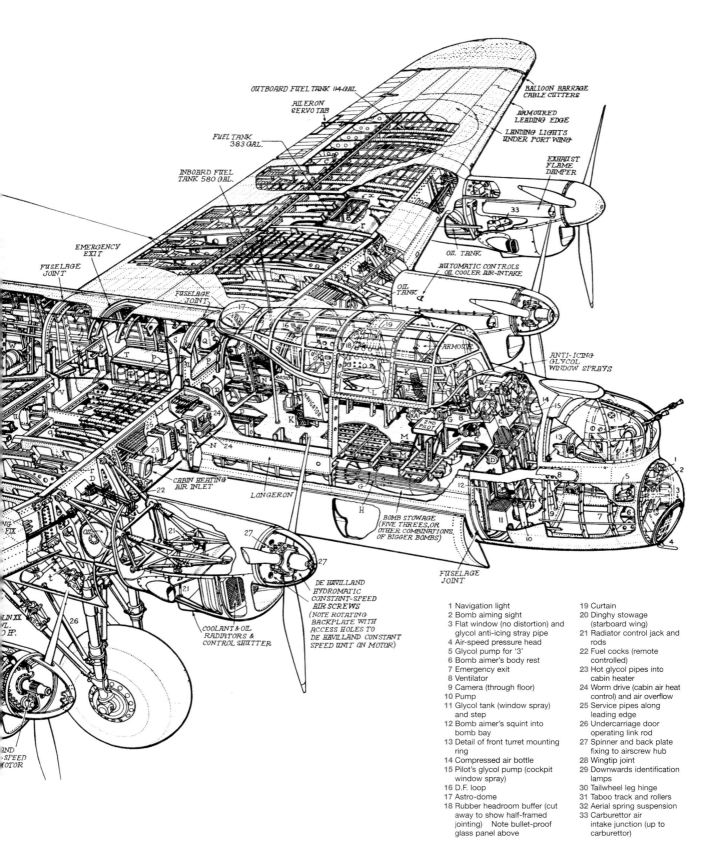

OUTBOARD FUEL TANK 114 GAL.

AILERON SERVO TAB

FUEL TANK 383 GAL.

INBOARD FUEL TANK 580 GAL.

BALLOON BARRAGE CABLE CUTTERS

ARMOURED LEADING EDGE

LANDING LIGHTS UNDER PORT WING

EXHAUST FLAME DAMPER

OIL TANK

AUTOMATIC CONTROLS OIL COOLER AIR-INTAKE

OIL TANK

ANTI-ICING GLYCOL WINDOW SPRAYS

EMERGENCY EXIT

FUSELAGE JOINT

FUSELAGE JOINT

ARMOUR

2ND PILOT

NAVIGATOR

RADIO

CABIN HEATING AIR INLET

LONGERON

BOMB STOWAGE (FIVE THREES, OR OTHER COMBINATIONS OF BIGGER BOMBS)

FUSELAGE JOINT

DE HAVILLAND HYDROMATIC CONSTANT-SPEED AIR SCREWS

(NOTE ROTATING BACKPLATE WITH ACCESS HOLES TO DE HAVILLAND CONSTANT SPEED UNIT ON MOTOR)

COOLANT & OIL RADIATORS & CONTROL SHUTTER

1 Navigation light
2 Bomb aiming sight
3 Flat window (no distortion) and glycol anti-icing stray pipe
4 Air-speed pressure head
5 Glycol pump for '3'
6 Bomb aimer's body rest
7 Emergency exit
8 Ventilator
9 Camera (through floor)
10 Pump
11 Glycol tank (window spray) and step
12 Bomb aimer's squint into bomb bay
13 Detail of front turret mounting ring
14 Compressed air bottle
15 Pilot's glycol pump (cockpit window spray)
16 D.F. loop
17 Astro-dome
18 Rubber headroom buffer (cut away to show half-framed jointing) Note bullet-proof glass panel above

19 Curtain
20 Dinghy stowage (starboard wing)
21 Radiator control jack and rods
22 Fuel cocks (remote controlled)
23 Hot glycol pipes into cabin heater
24 Worm drive (cabin air heat control) and air overflow
25 Service pipes along leading edge
26 Undercarriage door operating link rod
27 Spinner and back plate fixing to airscrew hub
28 Wingtip joint
29 Downwards identification lamps
30 Tailwheel leg hinge
31 Taboo track and rollers
32 Aerial spring suspension
33 Carburettor air intake junction (up to carburettor)

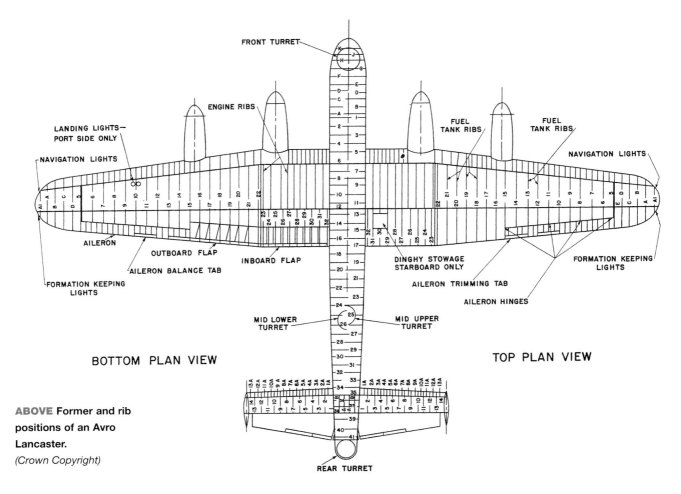

FRONT TURRET

ENGINE RIBS

LANDING LIGHTS—
PORT SIDE ONLY

NAVIGATION LIGHTS

FUEL
TANK RIBS

FUEL
TANK RIBS

NAVIGATION LIGHTS

AILERON

OUTBOARD FLAP

AILERON BALANCE TAB

INBOARD FLAP

DINGHY STOWAGE
STARBOARD ONLY

FORMATION KEEPING
LIGHTS

FORMATION KEEPING
LIGHTS

AILERON TRIMMING TAB

AILERON HINGES

MID LOWER
TURRET

MID UPPER
TURRET

BOTTOM PLAN VIEW

TOP PLAN VIEW

REAR TURRET

ABOVE Former and rib positions of an Avro Lancaster.
(Crown Copyright)

The fuselage

Because of its size the fuselage is divided into five sections. These are the nose, front centre section, centre section, rear centre section and rear fuselage. These sections, when bolted together, form the main fuselage. This is a stressed skin monocoque construction, built up with transverse channel section formers (frames), stiffened by fore and aft stringers that connect to the formers to provide the framework.

RIGHT Inside of the fuselage looking forward from the rear of the bomb bay, showing the frame construction and internal fittings.
(Paul Blackah/ Crown Copyright)

FAR RIGHT Close-up view of the frame construction.
(Paul Blackah/ Crown Copyright)

This framework is covered with alclad (a light aluminium alloy) sheet, the majority being 22 SWG but in some places 16 SWG. This is riveted to the formers and stringers with dome-head rivets.

The completed fuselage is made up of 51 formers, which are identified by numbers and letters. Formers 1–41 proceed aft from the first complete former in the front centre portion. Formers A–K (excluding letter I, which is not used due to its similarity to the number 1) proceed forward from that point.

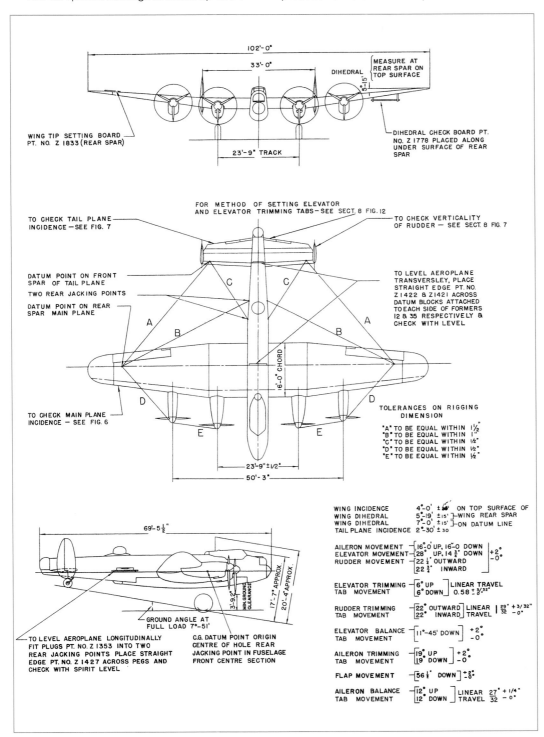

The nose

The nose section houses the front FN5 turret and the bomb aimer's position, and extends back as far as the joint at former E.

Front centre section

The front centre section runs from the joint at former E to the joint at former 6. This houses the pilot's, navigator's and radio operator's stations.

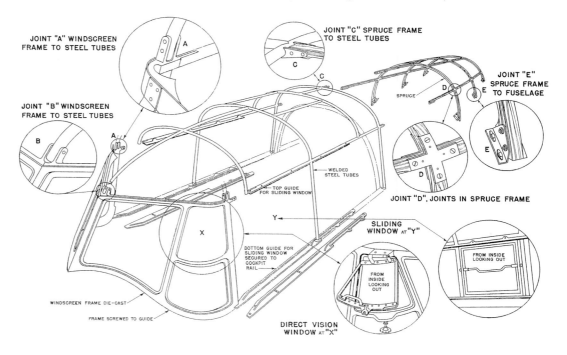

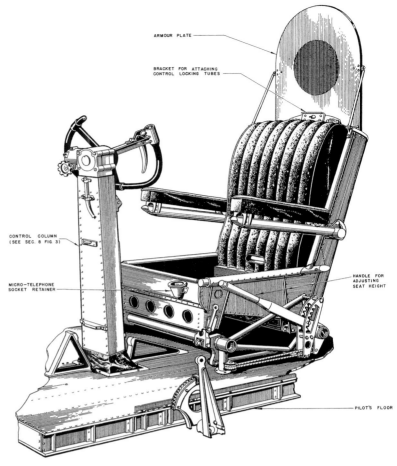

ARMOUR PLATE

BRACKET FOR ATTACHING
CONTROL LOCKING TUBES

CONTROL COLUMN
(SEE SEC. 8 FIG. 3)

MICRO-TELEPHONE
SOCKET RETAINER

HANDLE FOR
ADJUSTING
SEAT HEIGHT

PILOT'S FLOOR

Centre section

This serves as a rest compartment, running from the joint at former 6 to the joint at former 12.

The centre section of the fuselage is built on the front and rear spars of the mainplane.

ABOVE Pilot's seat.
(Crown Copyright)

ABOVE LEFT
Electrical distribution panel situated on the starboard side, forward of the rear spar. *(Paul Blackah/ Crown Copyright)*

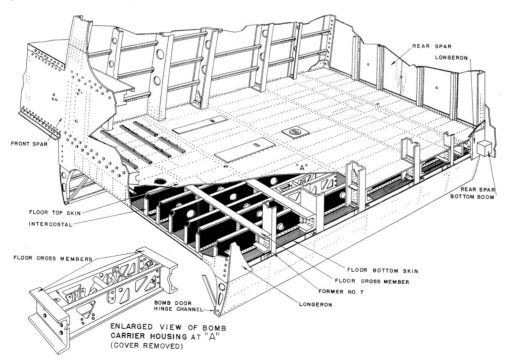

REAR SPAR

LONGERON

FRONT SPAR

REAR SPAR
BOTTOM BOOM

"A"

FLOOR TOP SKIN

INTERCOSTAL

FLOOR CROSS MEMBERS

FLOOR BOTTOM SKIN
FLOOR CROSS MEMBER
FORMER NO. 7

LONGERON

BOMB DOOR
HINGE CHANNEL

ENLARGED VIEW OF BOMB
CARRIER HOUSING AT "A"
(COVER REMOVED)

LEFT Centre section
floor construction.
(Crown Copyright)

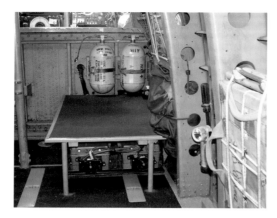

RIGHT Situated behind the front spar are the emergency air blow-down bottles for the flaps and undercarriage. *(Paul Blackah/ Crown Copyright)*

FAR RIGHT TOP Situated high on the port side of the fuselage behind the front spar is the aircraft's hydraulic tank, filter and automatic cut-out valve ('acov'). *(Paul Blackah/ Crown Copyright)*

RIGHT The rear wing spar joining the centre section of the fuselage. *(Paul Blackah/ Crown Copyright)*

FAR RIGHT Behind the rear spar is the flap jack, seen here with its end covers fitted. *(Paul Blackah/ Crown Copyright)*

BELOW The mid-upper turret shown with seat hanging down, step stowed to the left and white bags for collecting spent ammunition cases. *(Paul Blackah/Crown Copyright)*

RIGHT Internal view of the mid-upper turret. *(Paul Blackah/Crown Copyright)*

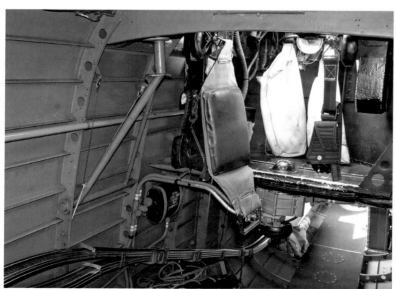

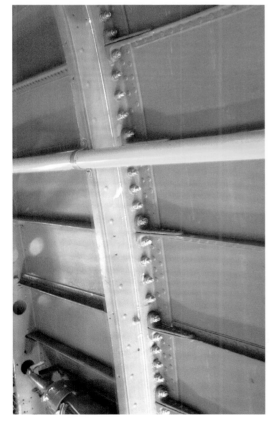

Rear centre section

This runs from the joint at former 12 to the joint at former 27 and houses the FN50 mid-upper turret.

Rear fuselage

The rear fuselage runs from the joint at former 27 to the end of the fuselage (former 41), and houses the tail unit and the rear FN121 turret.

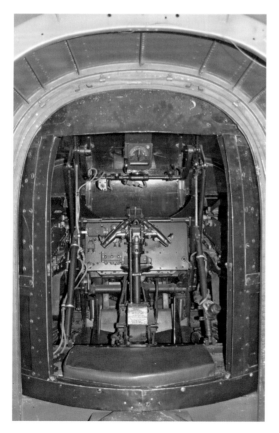

Bomb doors

The two bomb doors run from just aft of the joint at former E to former 22. They are made up of a central spar with nose and main ribs and are covered with a thin alloy skin (24 gauge). Each door has an hydraulic jack attachment at each end.

The tail unit

The tail unit consists of a port and starboard tailplane to which are attached the fins, rudders and elevators. The two tailplanes are bolted together at the centre of the fuselage at formers 35 and 38. The tailplane is built up of a front and rear spar with 16 ribs that are braced with stringers; these are then covered with alclad skin panels.

The fins

The fins are built up from front, rear, and intermediate fin posts, with vertical stringers, intercostals and ten horizontal ribs. The fin posts are stiffened by steel liners, which are riveted to them. The rear fin posts have

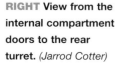

LEFT General view
of the tail unit, with
the elevators seen in
the lowered position
that would cause the
aircraft to adopt a
nose-down attitude in
flight. *(Jarrod Cotter)*

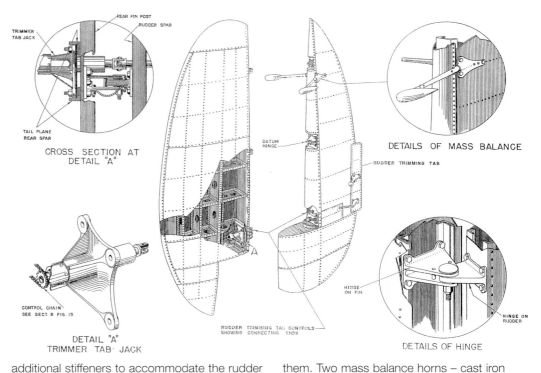

REAR FIN POST
RUDDER SPAR
TRIMMER
TAB JACK
TAIL PLANE
REAR SPAR
CROSS SECTION AT
DETAIL "A"

DATUM
HINGE

DETAILS OF MASS BALANCE
RUDDER TRIMMING TAB

CONTROL CHAIN
SEE SECT. 8 FIG.13

DETAIL "A"
TRIMMER TAB JACK

RUDDER TRIMMING TAB CONTROLS
SHOWING CONNECTING ENDS

HINGE
ON FIN

HINGE ON
RUDDER

DETAILS OF HINGE

additional stiffeners to accommodate the rudder hinge brackets, which are bolted onto the rear face. The whole of the fin structure is covered with an alclad skin.

The rudders

The rudders are of similar construction to the fins, to which three hinge assemblies attach

them. Two mass balance horns – cast iron weights – are supported by tubular arms bolted between ribs 9 and 10. Each rudder has a trim tab fitted to it.

The elevators

Each elevator consists of 16 main ribs, which are welded to the main tubular spar, and light

RIGHT **Starboard fin
and rudder. The fin is
fixed rigid, while the
rudder is the movable
portion at the rear.
Rudders affect the
yaw of the aircraft,
ie the left and right
movement in the
horizontal plane. Note
also the mass balance
horn towards the top
of the rudder, and the
trim tab at the bottom
trailing edge.**
*(Paul Blackah/
Crown Copyright)*

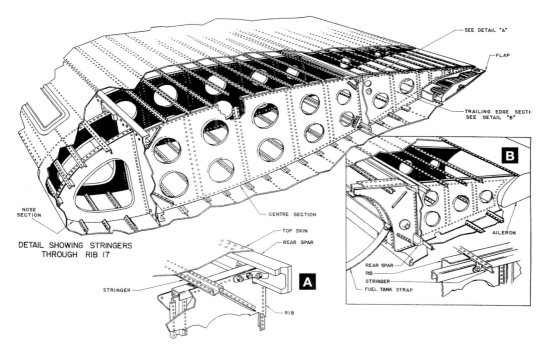

LEFT Typical
mainplane section.
(Crown Copyright)

alloy nose ribs, which are riveted to lugs and
then welded onto the main tubular spar. The
whole unit is then covered with a light alloy
skin, which is riveted in place. The elevators are
connected inside the fuselage by means of a
steel torque tube; each has a trimming tab and
a balance tab. Early production Lancasters had
fabric-covered elevators.

The wings

The Lancaster mainplane runs from the
starboard wingtip, through the centre
section (including the fuselage), and ends
at the port wingtip. Each side is made up of
33 ribs, numbered 5–32 and lettered E–A1.
Of these, E–A1 form each wingtip, 5–22 form

BELOW The Lancaster
has a 102ft wingspan,
evident from this
unusual vantage point.
*(Neil Clegg/
Crown Copyright)*

the outer planes, and 23–32 make up the centre section.

The outer and centre sections have forward, rear, upper and lower main spar booms. The outer section is attached to the centre section by means of a forged shackle that is bolted to the spar booms.

For transportation purposes the mainplane is broken down into the following sections: centre plane, both port and starboard trailing edge of the centre plane, port and starboard outer plane, trailing edge of the port and starboard outer plane, port and starboard wing tips, port and starboard ailerons, port and starboard flaps, and the centre plane hinged leading edge, port and starboard.

The undercarriage

The undercarriage consists of two retractable main legs and a fixed tail leg. The main undercarriage is made up of two shock absorber struts, a K-strut and an axle. Together these items are known as the panel assembly. The panel assembly is attached to the airframe by two large bolts, which attach to the undercarriage support beams mounted on the front spar.

Attached to the panel assembly are two drag stays. These are also connected to the lower rear spar of the mainplane. Two retraction jacks, attached to the drag stays close to the centre point, enable the undercarriage to retract rearwards and upwards into the nacelle, where they lock into place.

Shock absorber struts are oil and air filled (1,000psi) to provide damping action to the aircraft on landing.

ABOVE Another unusual viewpoint of the Lancaster's wing. *(Jarrod Cotter)*

TOP RIGHT Newly completed skin repair to port wingtip. *(Crown Copyright)*

RIGHT Shackle plate and bolts that hold the outer wing to the centre section. *(Crown Copyright)*

RIGHT Skin repair work to the underside of a wing. *(Crown Copyright)*

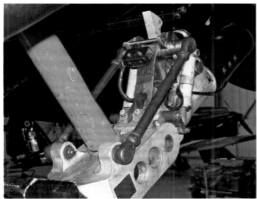

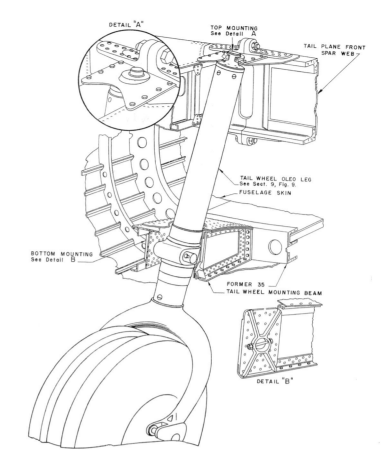

DETAIL "A"

TOP MOUNTING
See Detail A

TAIL PLANE FRONT
SPAR WEB

TAIL WHEEL OLEO LEG
See Sect. 9, Fig. 9.

FUSELAGE SKIN

BOTTOM MOUNTING
See Detail B

FORMER 35
TAIL WHEEL MOUNTING BEAM

DETAIL "B"

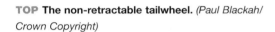

TOP The non-retractable tailwheel. *(Paul Blackah/ Crown Copyright)*

ABOVE Drag stay locking mechanism shown when the main undercarriage leg is locked down. The red tube is the undercarriage ground lock. *(Paul Blackah/Crown Copyright)*

TOP RIGHT Tailwheel mounting inside the rear fuselage. *(Crown Copyright)*

RIGHT The outboard undercarriage jack (upper) and drag stay (lower). The orange item is the number 2 fuel tank.

The tail leg is non-retractable and is oil and air filled (670psi). It is a self-centring unit with the added assistance of an anti-shimmy device fitted externally. This stops the tail end from violently shaking on landing and take-off. It is fitted into a socket behind the centre joint of the tailplane upper boom, where it is also attached by a pin to the lower tailwheel mounting beam, which is a box section fitted in the rear fuselage, located under the tailplane.

How to remove a Lancaster wheel to replace a worn brake unit

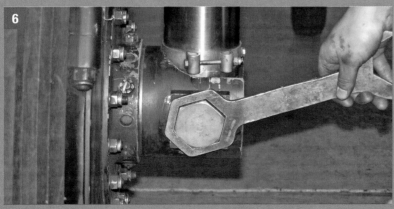

1 Jack adaptor access panel removed

2 Senior Aircraftman Barlow fitting the jack adaptor in place

3 25-tonne jack being positioned

4 Jack in position ready to lift aircraft

5 The tail-wheel is chocked prior to arc lifting the aircraft

6 The axle bolt nut is undone and removed

7 With the aircraft lifted, the wheel chariot is positioned

8 The chariot is lifted, allowing the axle to clear the oleos

9 Senior Aircraftman Barlow disconnecting the brake hoses

10 The axle bolts are then removed

11 Axle bolt nearly removed

12 The wheel is removed, allowing the brake unit to be replaced

13 With the wheel removed you can clearly see where the bolt fits

14 Lancaster brake unit removed from wheel. You can see the brake pads, retaining plates and springs.

(All Paul Blackah/ Crown Copyright)

The Rolls-Royce Merlin engine

The Rolls-Royce Merlin engines fitted to the Lancaster should be the Merlin XX series. However, the BBMF Lancaster operates using Merlin 25, 225 and 500 engines. These are very similar in specification, and for the purpose of this book we will take a closer look at the Merlin 25.

The Merlin 25 is a 12-cylinder, 60°, V12 liquid-cooled engine. It has a compression ratio of 6:1 and its dry weight is 1,430lb.

The two-piece cylinder block is cast from aluminium alloy. There are six cylinder liners in each block, manufactured from high carbon steel. Each piston has three compression and two oil scraper rings. The connecting rods are nickel steel forgings, machined to H-sections. The one-piece six-throw crankshaft is machine forged from chrome-molybdenum steel. The crankcase is cast from aluminium alloy. Two inlet and two exhaust valves are fitted to each cylinder head and each exhaust valve has a sodium-cooled stem.

Cylinders

The two cylinder assemblies, mainly the right- and left-hand blocks, are known as the A and B blocks respectively. Each comprises six cylinders, the upper camshaft drive unit and the camshaft and rocker mechanism, which operates the valves incorporated in the cylinders. Each block consists of a separate alloy skirt, head and six detachable wet steel liners which, when bolted together, form the cylinder block proper. In addition to providing part of the coolant jacket, the head also forms the roofs of the six combustion chambers.

Cylinder liners

Each cylinder liner is shouldered and spigotted at the upper end to enter its respective recess in the bottom of the cylinder head. The cylinder liner is also provided with a sealing ring at its lower end to form a joint with the crankcase, to which it is drawn by the cylinder holding-down studs.

Cylinder block covers

The covers are secured to their respective cylinder blocks by studs and nuts, with a gasket between the two contacting faces. The main difference between the A and B covers is that the latter incorporates an engine speed indicator drive whilst the former is plain.

Valves

There are two inlet and exhaust valves per cylinder. Both valves are of the trumpet type and have satellite-ended stems. The valve guides are cast iron for the inlet and phosphor-bronze for the exhaust. The valves are not interchangeable. Each valve guide is pressed into its respective bore in the cylinder block until a conical collar near its top end is seated on, and is flush with, the roof of the cylinder block.

Camshaft

A single central camshaft for each cylinder block is mounted in pedestal brackets and operates both inlet and exhaust valves through rockers fitted with adjustable tappets. The camshafts, which are similar for both blocks, are driven from the wheel case by inclined shafts ending in bevel pinions, which mesh with bevel wheels at the end of each camshaft.

Camshaft auxiliary drive

The air compressor and hydraulic pumps for the turrets are mounted on the rear ends of the A and B cylinder heads. Both are driven from the spur gear wheels attached to the camshaft-driven bevel wheels.

Pistons

The pistons are attached to the connecting rods by fully floating gudgeon pins. The connecting rods are of the forked and plain type, the forked rod being fitted to the B-side of the engine.

The pistons are machined from light alloy forgings and are fitted with three compression rings above and one grooved scraper ring below the gudgeon pin. The gudgeon pins are made from hollow steel and are retained in the piston by spring wire circlips. A pair of oil holes are drilled obliquely and upwards towards the centre to meet in the metal above each gudgeon pin bore to assist in cooling the piston.

Crankcase

The crankcase consists of two halves bolted together. The upper portion incorporates the

Rolls-Royce Merlin 25.

(Paul Blackah/Crown Copyright)

1 Camshaft cover
2 Generator housing, generator not fitted
3 Magneto
4 Reduction gear
5 Ignition harness
6 Carburettor
7 Two-speed single stage supercharger
8 Coolant pump
9 Magneto
10 Oil control valve
11 CSU oil filter

Diagram showing all the installation connections for a Rolls-Royce Merlin engine. *(Crown Copyright)*

1 Coolant outlets
2 De-icing connection to propeller
3 Vacuum pump inlet
4 Vacuum pump return
5 Engine mounting feet
6 Oil pressure gauge connection
7 Oil thermometer gauge connection
8 De-icing inlet connection
9 Coolant inlet to cylinder
10 Dowty pump drain
11 Oil inlet
12 Coolant pump outlet
13 Coolant pump inlet
14 Starter motor terminals
15 Supercharger bearing vent
16 Slow-running cut-off lever
17 Oil outlet
18 Constant-speed propeller governor unit
19 Wheelcase breather vent
20 Magneto earthing connection
21 Magneto booster coil connection
22 Throttle control levers (alternative)
23 Boost gauge connection
24 Cabin heater connection
25 Haywood air compressor outlet
26 I.A.E. pump delivery
27 I.A.E. pump drain
28 I.A.E. pump inlet
29 Fuel priming connection
30 Propeller shaft
31 Crankcase breather
32 Engine starting handle
33 Fire extinguishing system inlet
34 R.A.E. air compressor oil inlet
35 R.A.E. air compressor air inlet
36 R.A.E. air compressor air & oil outlet
37 Engine-speed indicator drive
38 R.A.E. air compressor drain
39 Boost control cut-out lever
40 Two-speed supercharger control
41 Fuel pump drain
42 Fuel pump inlet
43 Fuel priming connection to fuel pump
44 Oil dilution connection
45 Fuel pressure gauge connection
46 Lockheed pump drain
47 Electric generator terminals
48 Electric generator air cooling inlet
49 Electric generator air cooling outlet

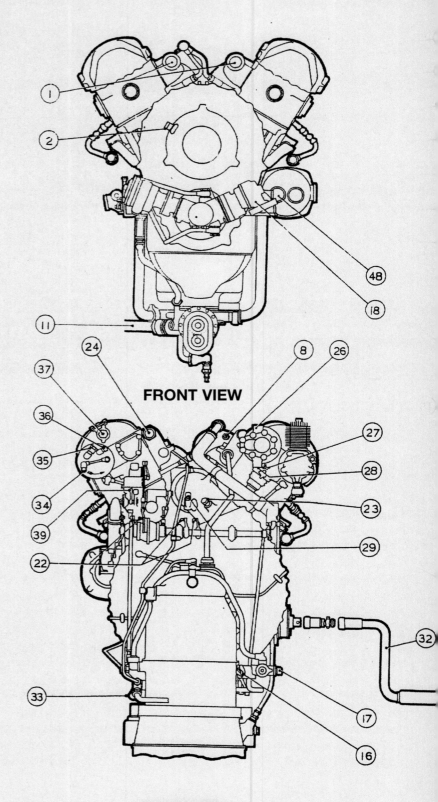

FRONT VIEW

REAR VIEW

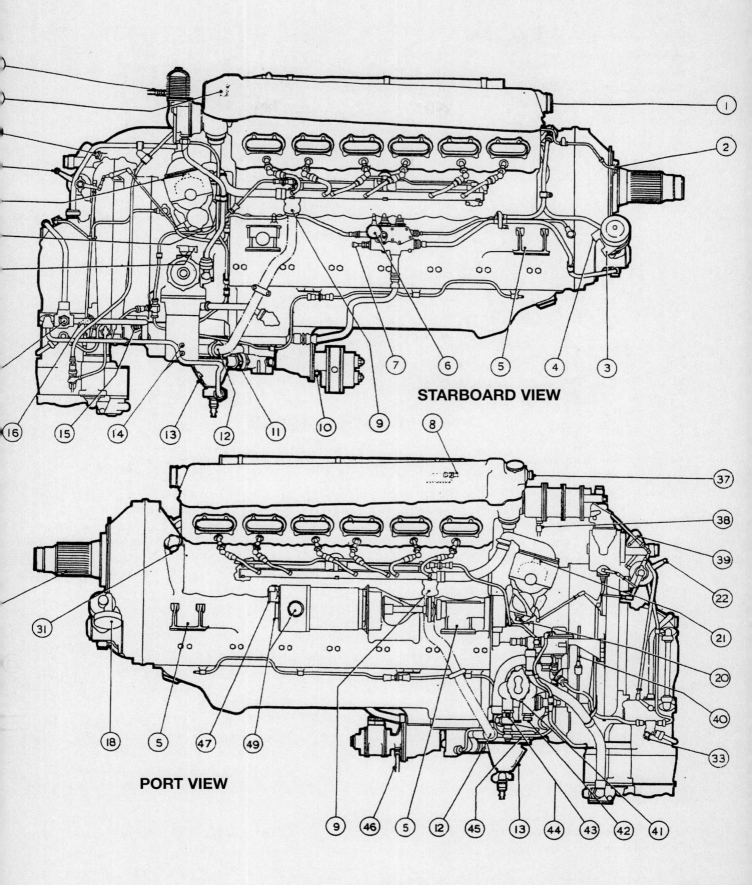

STARBOARD VIEW

PORT VIEW

RIGHT Front of
Merlin propeller shaft,
reduction gear and
constant speed unit
(CSU). *(Paul Blackah/
Crown Copyright)*

rear half of the reduction gear housing at its
front end, and has a facing and spigot at the
rear end to which the wheel case is attached.
The lower portion incorporates the scavenge
pumps, filters, and the mounting for the
hydraulic system pump. This is only fitted to the
number 2 and 3 engines.

Reduction gear

The reduction gear is of a single-spur layshaft
type and is housed partly in a casing bolted
to the front end of the crankcase and partly in
the crankcase itself. The casing is located on
the crankcase by means of a spigot concentric
with the propeller shaft. The driving pinion
is concentric with, and is driven by, a short
coupling shaft from the crankshaft. All these
shafts run in roller bearings, the propeller shaft
having, in addition, a thrustable ball bearing,
enabling the engine to be used with tractor
(pulling) or pusher propeller. A dual-drive unit
is fitted to the reduction gear cover for the
purpose of driving the propeller constant
speed unit (CSU) and vacuum pump unit,
which are both bolted to it. The vacuum

pump is used for the operation of certain
navigational instruments.

Wheel case assembly

The wheel case is bolted to the rear end of the
crankcase and carries the magnetos, coolant
pump, generator drive, electric turning gear and
fuel pump unit. It houses the spring-drive unit
and certain shafts through which the magnetos,
camshafts, electric generator, fuel, oil and
coolant pumps are driven.

Coolant pump

The coolant pump is of the bottom-fed
centrifugal type and serves each cylinder block
from a separate outlet.

Fuel pump

The fuel pump unit, mounted on the facing on
the port side of the wheel case, consists of
two separate pumps operating in parallel. Each
pump is capable of operating independently of
the other and each is of sufficient capacity to
supply more than the maximum amount of
fuel required.

LEFT Merlin 25 viewed from the rear, showing the supercharger unit and carburettor clearly. *(Paul Blackah/ Crown Copyright)*

Electrical generator drive

The electrical generator is mounted upon a cast light alloy right-angled bracket that is located on the left-hand side of the crankcase.

Supercharger

The two-speed, single-stage, liquid-cooled supercharger is of the high-speed centrifugal type, embodying a semi-shrouded impellor which is driven from the rear end of the crankshaft through a two-speed gear.

Carburetion

The SU twin-choke up-draught type Merlin carburettor fitted to this engine is, with the exception of the separate boost control unit, entirely self-contained and is arranged to be fully automatic in its functioning, with the result that the responsibilities of the pilot are reduced to their simplest form and the danger of engine damage resulting from incorrect setting is reduced.

The SU type Merlin AVT40/193, or 214 carburettor, embodies two complete carburettors in one unit. The flow of fuel through the left-hand carburettor main jet is directly controlled by the induction pressure-operated mixture control, whilst the right-hand jet is directly controlled by the atmospherically operated mixture control. Both these mixture controls are automatically controlled through linkwork by separate aneroid capsules incorporated on each side of the carburettor. The upper half of the carburettor casting is mounted on studs on the lower face of the supercharger intake elbow. A large specially shaped gasket is used at the joint faces to provide a gas-tight and fuel-tight joint.

Both the vertical intake passage and throttle barrels are coolant jacketed, these jackets being included in the coolant return from the B cylinder block to the inlet side of the coolant pump. A system of oil-heated throttle valves is also included to prevent freezing and to allow for a portion of the scavenge oil being directed through the hollow interior of the throttle valves before it is returned to the oil tank.

Ignition system

The ignition system comprises two magnetos, which are attached to the wheel case,

one on the left, and one on the right. Attached to these are the high-tension wiring harnesses for the spark plugs, which are metal screened and serve a dual purpose by acting as a collector for the induced field around the high tension wires and returning the resulting electrical current to earth, and also preventing radio interference. Each cylinder has two spark plugs – one magneto provides the spark for the inlet-side plugs and the other for the exhaust-side plugs. This ensures that if one magneto fails, the engine will still run using the other.

Engine lubrication system

There are four oil circuits in the lubrication system of the engine: the main pressure feed circuit; the low pressure feed circuit; the front sump scavenge circuit; and the rear sump scavenge circuit. The main and lower circuits are served by a single pressure pump and suitable relief valves, while each scavenge circuit is served by a separate scavenge pump.

Engine controls

The control lever for the throttle, airscrew and boost cut-out, together with the engine fuel

RIGHT Engine control details of the cockpit. *(Crown Copyright)*

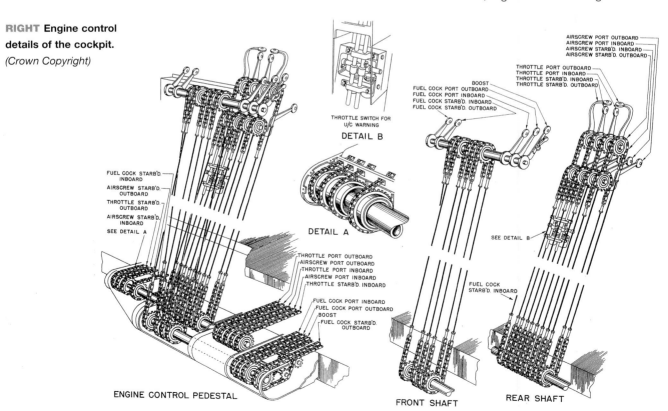

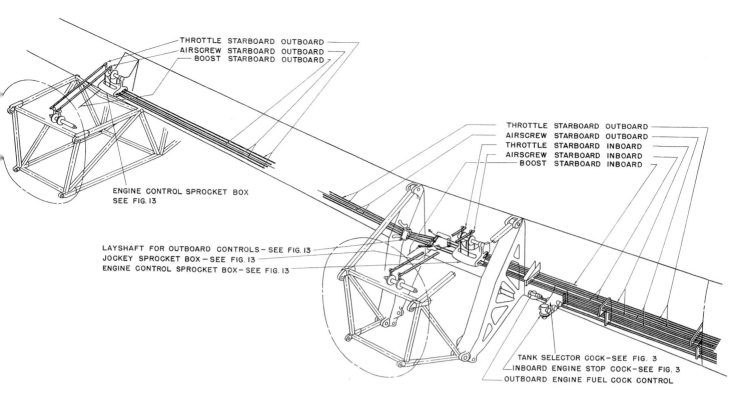

THROTTLE STARBOARD OUTBOARD
AIRSCREW STARBOARD OUTBOARD
BOOST STARBOARD OUTBOARD

THROTTLE STARBOARD OUTBOARD
AIRSCREW STARBOARD OUTBOARD
THROTTLE STARBOARD INBOARD
AIRSCREW STARBOARD INBOARD
BOOST STARBOARD INBOARD

ENGINE CONTROL SPROCKET BOX
SEE FIG. 13

LAYSHAFT FOR OUTBOARD CONTROLS—SEE FIG. 13
JOCKEY SPROCKET BOX—SEE FIG. 13
ENGINE CONTROL SPROCKET BOX—SEE FIG. 13

TANK SELECTOR COCK—SEE FIG. 3
INBOARD ENGINE STOP COCK—SEE FIG. 3
OUTBOARD ENGINE FUEL COCK CONTROL

cock controls, are mounted on a quadrant below the instrument panel. Chains and tie rods connect the control levers to the engine control boxes behind the engines. The inboard engine boxes are mounted on the front spar and the outboard engine boxes are located on brackets on the front spar.

ABOVE Engine and secondary control layout on the mainplane. *(Crown Copyright)*

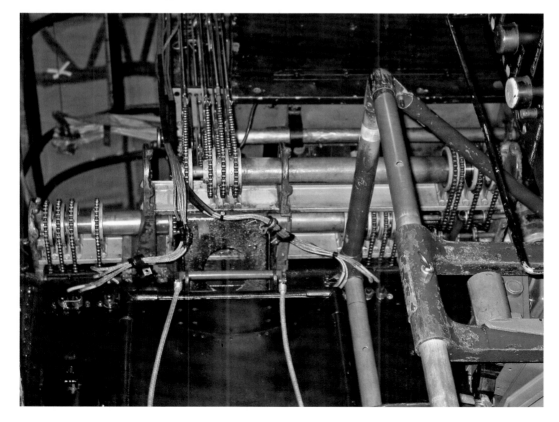

LEFT Covers removed to show the engine control workings of the main pedestal in the cockpit. *(Paul Blackah/ Crown Copyright)*

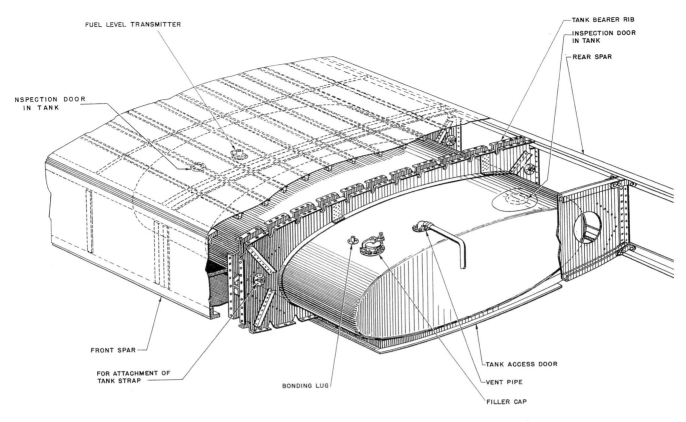

FUEL LEVEL TRANSMITTER

INSPECTION DOOR IN TANK

TANK BEARER RIB

INSPECTION DOOR IN TANK

REAR SPAR

FRONT SPAR

FOR ATTACHMENT OF TANK STRAP

BONDING LUG

TANK ACCESS DOOR

VENT PIPE

FILLER CAP

ABOVE Outboard fuel tank mounting. *(Crown Copyright)*

RIGHT Each wing has three fuel tanks fitted, which are retained by straps. *(Crown Copyright)*

FAR RIGHT Fuel tank bay with unit removed. *(Crown Copyright)*

RIGHT Here the fuel tank has its outer covering removed for maintenance work. *(Crown Copyright)*

FAR RIGHT Access panel open to the number 1 fuel tank filler cap. *(Paul Blackah/ Crown Copyright)*

Systems

Fuel system

The fuel system consists of separate port and starboard systems connected by a balance pipe. On each side of the fuselage, mounted in the mainplane, are three metal tanks, each fitted with an electric booster pump. Fuel is drawn by the engine pump or pumped by the booster pump from the tanks through non-return valves to the tank selector cocks. From here a supply is run to each engine.

The two inboard fuel tanks – the number 1 fuel tanks – hold 580 gallons each; the intermediate, or number 2 tanks, hold 383 gallons each; and the outboard, or number 3 tanks, holds 114 gallons each. Each tank is filled independently from the top of the wing.

On the BBMF's Lancaster only the number 3 tanks are fully filled and the fuel load never exceeds 1,000 gallons, with the rest of the fuel being evenly distributed throughout the other tanks. This is done to minimise fatigue and stress to the wings.

Cooling system

Each engine has its own independent cooling system. This comprises a header tank mounted behind the front cowling diaphragm, a radiator, attached below the engine, and a thermostat.

The system is operated under pressure, which is controlled by a thermostatic release valve at the top of the header tank. This valve limits the maximum pressure and provides a controlled escape of air, which allows for expansion at different temperatures. The temperature of the coolant is controlled by the thermostat, which allows the amount of airflow through the radiator dependent on the temperature. The coolant consists of 30 per cent glycol (AL3), and 70 per cent distilled water.

Oil system

The oil system also has an independent system for each engine. This comprises an oil tank mounted in the engine sub-frame and an oil cooler mounted below the engine. The main

BELOW PA474 stripped of its engine cowlings, showing the radiators hanging below each Merlin and the oil tanks behind the engines in the sub-frame.
(Crown Copyright)

feed pipe is taken from the filter in the oil tank and passes to the engine oil pump. The oil is returned via the oil cooler to the top of the oil tank. Each oil tank holds 37½ gallons of oil (OMD270).

Propellers

Four Hamilton Standard three-bladed metal propellers drive the aircraft. These are the later wide-blade versions rather than the thinner blades that were mostly used during World War Two. Each propeller has the capacity to 'feather', which means that if there is an engine problem and the engine has to shut down, the individual blades can turn to 'fully fine' so that no drag is created.

Electrical system

Two generators drive the 28v electrical system on the number 2 and 3 engines. This system operates the lights, internal and external, instruments, radios, intercom and navigation aids. It is backed up by four 24v batteries located behind the front spar.

Hydraulic system

Two hydraulic pumps fitted to the inboard engines operate the hydraulic system. Pipework from the two pumps runs to the hydraulic reservoir situated to the rear of the front spar, to an accumulator and an automatic cut-out valve which regulates the hydraulic pressure to around 850psi. This system operates the undercarriage, the bomb doors and the flaps.

A selector valve on the right-hand side of the pilot's seat operates the undercarriage system. This selector is always in either the UP or DOWN position. When a selection is made fluid is delivered under pressure through the selector to the undercarriage jacks.

The bomb doors are controlled by a similar selector valve positioned on the left-hand side of the pilot's seat. When the lever is pushed down the doors open and when it is pulled up they close. The doors are operated by four hydraulic jacks, one at the front and one at the rear of each door.

A single-cylinder jack, mounted in the fuselage behind the rear spar, operates the flaps. The piston rod of this jack extends outwards through both end covers; these are

then connected by universal jointed links to push-pull tubes, sliding in bushes, in the trailing edge of the mainplane. A series of short links then connects the flaps to the push-pull tubes.

A handle to the right of the pilot's seat, and a control valve mounted below the pilot's floor, govern the raising and lowering of the flaps. This unit has a neutral position, at which the handle is normally set. When the handle is moved to the down position oil is supplied to the downside of the jack so the flaps go down. After reaching the required position the handle is returned to neutral, thereby stopping the flow of oil.

Pneumatic system

The pneumatic system is operated by two Heyward compressors, which are fitted to the inboard engines. These supply pressure through a pressure-regulating valve, set at 450psi, to an air bottle situated behind the nose turret. This system operates the brakes and the radiator flaps.

A lever on the pilot and co-pilot's control column operates the brakes. This lever is cable-linked to the brake control valve and, when applied, air from the brake control valve inflates the brake bags to 120psi.

Flying controls

The pilot and the co-pilot operate all the flying controls. These include: ailerons, elevators, rudders, aileron trim, elevator trim, rudder trim and flaps. The ailerons are operated by a series of cable, chains, tie-rods and control tubes. The system runs along the port side of the fuselage and at the rear wing centre section it enters the port and starboard mainplanes, where it connects to the aileron outer wing bell crank. From there it travels to the aileron input rod and onto the aileron, which is a metal framework covered with Irish linen.

The elevator and rudder are operated by control rods that run down the port side of the fuselage to the tailplane where they connect to the controls, which are of metal construction.

All the trim systems are cable-operated (5cwt) to a screw jack, which then connects via an operating rod to the trim tabs.

ABOVE **Engine controls.** *(RAF Coningsby Photographic Section/ Crown Copyright)*

1 Fuel master cocks
2 Throttles
3 Constant speed unit controls
4 Boost cut-out lever
5 Pilot's control yoke
6 Co-pilot's control yoke
7 Pilot's rudder pedals
8 Co-pilot's rudder pedals
9 Rudder control lock in place
10 Control column

LEFT **Captain's control yoke. Note brake lever on the left-hand side.** *(RAF Coningsby Photographic Section/ Crown Copyright)*

The instrument panel of the Battle of Britain Memorial Flight's Lancaster I PA474.
(RAF Coningsby Photographic Section/ Crown Copyright)

1 Air speed
   indicator
2 Artificial horizon
3 Rate of climb
   indicator
4 Altimeter

5 Directional indicator
6 Turn and slip
   indicator
7 Accelerometer
8 Undercarriage
   indicator

9 Compass (P10)
10 Cockpit lights
11 Gyro compass
   remote indicator
12 Magneto
   switches

13 Boost indicators

14 RPM indicators

15 Engine start
buttons

16 Boost coil
switch

17 Fire indication test
button (guarded)

18 Flap indicator
switch

19 Vacuum indicator

20 Flap indicator

21 Vacuum system
changeover switch
(this works off the
number 2/3 engine)

22 Propeller feathering
buttons

23 Fire indication
lights

24 Extinguisher
buttons

25 Air system and
brake gauge

26 Identification
light Morse
switches

27 Engine radiator
shutter switches

28 VHF radio

RIGHT Close-up of the left-hand side of the instrument panel. *(RAF Coningsby Photographic Section/ Crown Copyright)*

RIGHT Centre of the instrument panel. *(RAF Coningsby Photographic Section/ Crown Copyright)*

RIGHT Right-hand side of the instrument panel. *(RAF Coningsby Photographic Section/ Crown Copyright)*

FAR LEFT Aileron, rudder and elevator trim wheels. The undercarriage selector lever and safety bolt are in red. The safety bolt prevents accidental operation of the undercarriage. *(Paul Blackah/ Crown Copyright)*

LEFT Aileron control rod linkage on rear spar. *(Paul Blackah/ Crown Copyright)*

LEFT Elevator and rudder control rods on fuselage side. *(Paul Blackah/ Crown Copyright)*

LEFT Ailerons with fabric removed showing the ribs and trailing edge.

ABOVE Six of the
eight Browning 0.303in
machine-guns installed
in PA474's turrets
pointing rearwards.
(Jarrod Cotter)

Turrets

The Lancaster was usually fitted with three turrets, although some had a fourth or mid-lower turret, positioned underneath the aircraft to the rear of the bomb doors. This would carry two Browning 0.303in guns with 1,000 rounds of ammunition. Each turret had its own hydraulic system, to enable the others to function should one be hit in action; this comprised a hydraulic pump, reservoir and recuperator. The BBMF Lancaster is fitted with the following turrets, although the hydraulic systems have been disabled and the turrets can only rotate when manually operated.

Nose turret

The FN5 nose turret was fitted with two Browning 0.303in machine guns, which held 1,000 rounds of ammunition per gun. Once the air gunner was in situ he was able to rotate through 190° by the use of two control handles. The handles also contained the triggers for the firing mechanism.

Mid-upper turret

The FN50 mid-upper turret was also fitted with two Browning 0.303in machine guns which each held 1,000 rounds of ammunition. To gain access to the turret a step was stowed on the inside of the fuselage, which swung into position when unclipped. Once the gunner was inside the turret the hammock-type seat was then clipped into position. The turret could rotate through 360°. In order to protect the tail unit from damage during firing there was a failsafe mechanism comprising 'taboo arms' that ran on a track fitted to the fairing around the turret. This enabled the air gunner to concentrate on firing without worrying about shooting his own tail off.

ABOVE PA474's nose, with the FN5 front gun turret prominent. *(Jarrod Cotter)*

LEFT The FN50 mid-upper turret. Note the 'taboo arms' below the guns. *(Jarrod Cotter)*

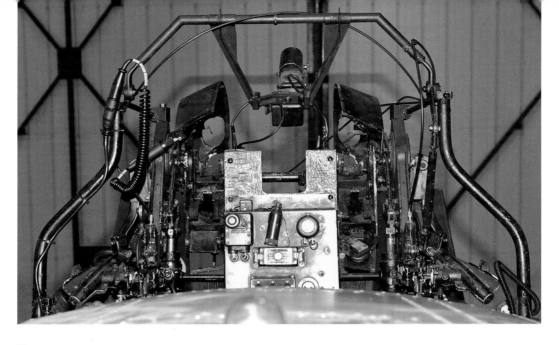

Rear turret

The FN121 rear turret was fitted with four Browning 0.303in machine guns, which were fed ammunition from stainless steel tracks that ran from two ammunition boxes attached to the floor at formers 20–22. The tracks ran either side of the fuselage and together could supply 2,500 rounds for each of the four guns. The turret could rotate through 190° and was operated in the same manner as the other turrets. Once inside the turret the air gunner closed two doors behind him, which prevented him from falling out when the turret was rotated.

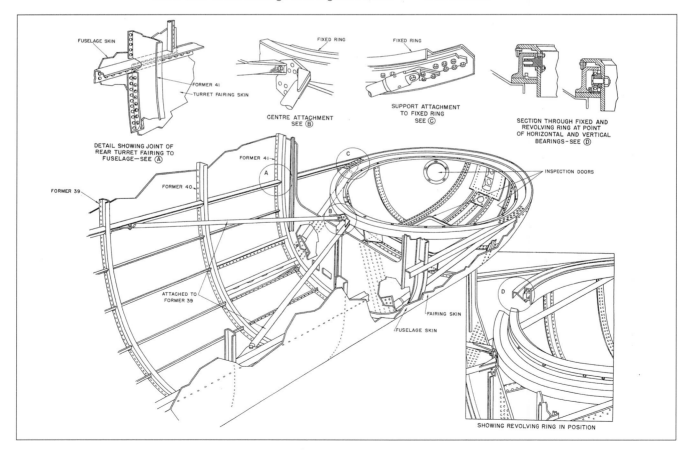

LEFT External view
of the FN121 rear
turret, fitted with four
Browning 0.303in
machine guns.
*(Paul Blackah
/Crown Copyright)*

BELOW Turret
hydraulic circuit
diagram.
(Crown Copyright)

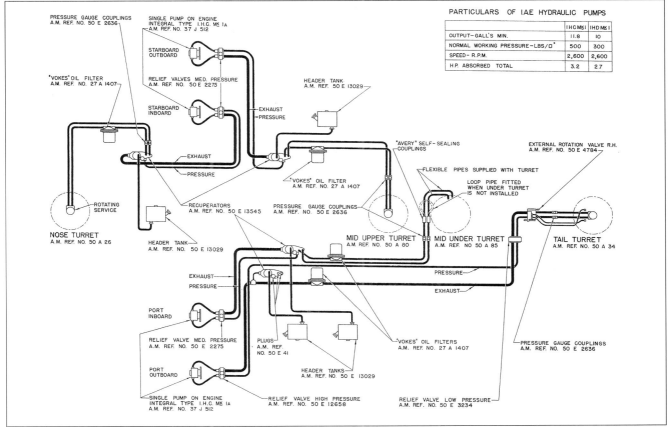

PRESSURE GAUGE COUPLINGS
A.M. REF. NO. 50 E 2636

SINGLE PUMP ON ENGINE
INTEGRAL TYPE I.H.C. MK IA
A.M. REF. NO. 37 J 512

STARBOARD
OUTBOARD

"VOKES" OIL FILTER
A.M. REF. NO. 27 A 1407

RELIEF VALVES MED. PRESSURE
A.M. REF. NO. 50 E 2275

STARBOARD
INBOARD

HEADER TANK
A.M. REF. 50 E 13029

EXHAUST
PRESSURE

EXHAUST
PRESSURE

ROTATING
SERVICE

RECUPERATORS
A.M. REF. NO. 50 E 13545

"VOKES" OIL FILTER
A.M. REF. NO. 27 A 1407

PRESSURE GAUGE COUPLINGS
A.M. REF. NO. 50 E 2636

"AVERY" SELF-SEALING
COUPLINGS

FLEXIBLE PIPES SUPPLIED WITH TURRET

LOOP PIPE FITTED
WHEN UNDER TURRET
IS NOT INSTALLED

EXTERNAL ROTATION VALVE R.H.
A.M. REF. NO. 50 E 4784

NOSE TURRET
A.M. REF. NO. 50 A 26

HEADER TANK
A.M. REF. NO. 50 E 13029

MID UPPER TURRET
A.M. REF. NO. 50 A 80

MID UNDER TURRET
A.M. REF. NO 50 A 85

TAIL TURRET
A.M. REF. NO. 50 A 34

EXHAUST
PRESSURE

PRESSURE

EXHAUST

PORT
INBOARD

RELIEF VALVE MED. PRESSURE
A.M. REF. NO. 50 E 2275

PLUGS
A.M. REF.
NO. 50 E 41

"VOKES" OIL FILTERS
A.M. REF. NO. 27 A 1407

PRESSURE GAUGE COUPLINGS
A.M. REF. NO. 50 E 2636

PORT
OUTBOARD

HEADER TANKS
A.M. REF. NO. 50 E 13029

SINGLE PUMP ON ENGINE
INTEGRAL TYPE I.H.C. MK IA
A.M. REF. NO. 37 J 512

RELIEF VALVE HIGH PRESSURE
A.M. REF. NO. 50 E 12658

RELIEF VALVE LOW PRESSURE
A.M. REF. NO. 50 E 3234

PARTICULARS OF I.A.E HYDRAULIC PUMPS

	IHC MK I	IHD MK I
OUTPUT—GALL'S MIN.	11.8	10
NORMAL WORKING PRESSURE—LBS/□"	500	300
SPEED— R.P.M.	2,600	2,600
H.P. ABSORBED TOTAL	3.2	2.7

Bomb bay and loads

The Lancaster's bomb bay could hold a variety of bomb loads depending on the operation to be carried out. The BBMF Lancaster has a 4,000lb bomb carrier and several 500lb bomb carriers fitted.

Bomb loading

Before loading bombs, the bomb cell doors were opened by pushing down the lever on the left-hand side of the pilot's seat. If the inboard engines were running the doors would open automatically, but if they weren't it was necessary to operate the emergency hand pump on the port wall of the fuselage just aft of spar 4. Safety brackets were then fitted to the four hydraulic jacks to prevent inadvertent closure of the doors whilst bomb-loading operations were in progress.

Standard bomb-loading winches were required, two 2,000lb winches being used to hoist the 4,000lb bomb. The adjustable crutches for the 4,000lb bomb were removed when other bomb loads were to be carried. A step-ladder was necessary in order to remove the bomb carriers, to make final adjustments, and to check that the bombs were in position.

Order of loading

Heavy bombs had to be loaded in the correct sequence. For this purpose each of the bomb gear housings (the arrangement of which depended on the type of bombs being carried) was numbered above and below the floor for ease of identification. Typical load options were:

- 14 x 250lb, 500lb or 1,000lb bombs (other than 500lb Marks I, II, III or IV AS bombs)
- 6 x mines or heavy bombs, plus smaller bombs
- 6 x 500lb AS bombs (Marks I, II and III only), plus smaller bombs
- 1 x 4,000lb bomb, plus smaller bombs

Note that in options B, C and D several smaller bombs were carried in addition to the main load, eg option D might comprise six 1,000lb and two 250lb bombs in addition to the 4,000lb bomb. The 14 bombs of option A,

however, represent a maximum load, with only the central bomb housing not being used. The 250lb or 500lb bombs or containers could be of the following types:

- 500lb GP bombs
- 500lb SAP bombs
- 250lb GP bombs
- 250lb SAP bombs
- 250lb LC bombs
- 250lb B bombs
- 250lb AS bombs
- Small-bomb containers

Although not important, it was more convenient to load the small bomb containers, the 500lb bombs and the 250lb bombs in that order. If the number of bombs to be fitted was less than 14, the centre housings would be used.

ABOVE Close-up of bomb slip.
(Paul Blackah/ Crown Copyright)

OPPOSITE Bomb bay, showing eleven 500lb bomb slips and the red crutches for the 4,000lb 'Cookie' bomb.
(Paul Blackah/ Crown Copyright)

THIS PAGE AND OPPOSITE
Various Lancaster bomb load configurations.
(Crown Copyright)

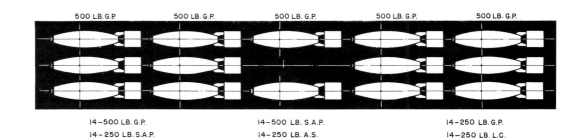

500 LB. G.P   500 LB. G.P.   500 LB. G.P.   500 LB. G.P.   500 LB. G.P.

14-500 LB. G.P.	14-500 LB. S.A.P.	14-250 LB. G.P.
14-250 LB. S.A.P.	14-250 LB. A.S.	14-250 LB. L.C.
14-250 LB.-B	14-250 LB. SMALL BOMB CONTAINERS	

ANY ONE OF THE ABOVE LOADINGS MAY BE USED

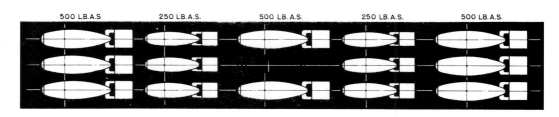

500 LB.A.S   250 LB.A.S.   500 LB.A.S.   250 LB.A.S.   500 LB.A.S.

8-500 LB. & 6-250 LB. A.S. (MK. IV ONLY)

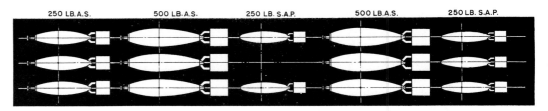

250 LB.A.S.   500 LB.A.S.   250 LB. S.A.P.   500 LB.A.S.   250 LB. S.A.P.

6-500 LB. & 3-250 LB.A.S. (MK. I, II & III) AND 5-250 LB. S.A.P.

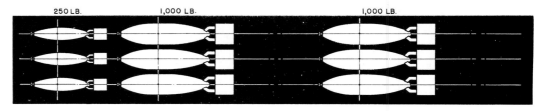

250 LB.   1,000 LB.   1,000 LB.

6-1,000 LB. & 3-250 LB. G.P.

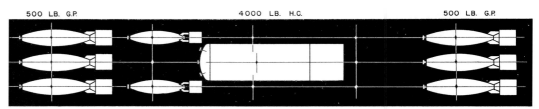

500 LB. G.P.   4000 LB. H.C.   500 LB. G.P.

1-4000 LB. H.C. -- 6-500 LB. G.P. & 2-250 LB. G.P. BOMBS

1500 LB. A MINES

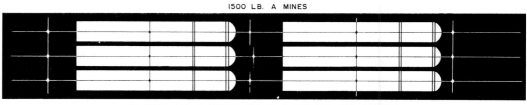

6-1500 LB. A MINES OR 6-2000 LB. H.C. BOMBS

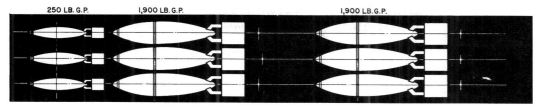

6-1900 LB. & 3-250 LB. G.P.

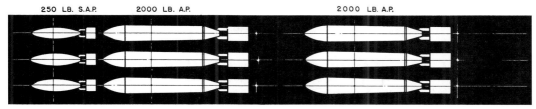

6-2000 LB. A.P. & 3-250 LB. S.A.P.

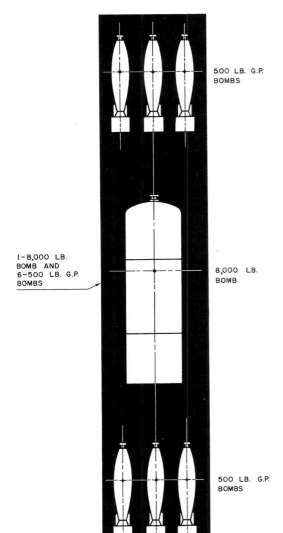

500lb and 600lb AS bombs

Fourteen 600lb AS bombs could be carried, but owing to the length of the 500lb AS bomb it was only possible to carry six Mark I, II or III or eight Mark IV bombs of this type. The sequence of loading was in reverse order to the numbering of the housings.

1,000lb bombs

Fourteen bombs of the following types could be carried and would be loaded in reverse order to the numbering of the housings:

- 1,000lb GP (short-tail type) bombs
- 1,000lb USA bombs
- 1,000lb MC bombs

However, only six of the long-tail GP type could be carried. The bombs at housings 12, 11, 10, 9, 8 and 7 would be loaded first, in that order.

Loading 250lb, 500lb or 1,000 lb bombs

Lancaster technical manual *AP2062A Volume I* provides full details of the loading procedure followed during the Second World War:

The following is the sequence of loading operations, using the 500lb standard winch for 250lb or 500lb bombs, and the 2,000lb standard winch for 1,000lb bombs:

(i). Open the bomb doors and fit the safety brackets.

(ii). Remove the cover plates from the bomb gear housings in the floor of the fuselage.

(iii). Using the small crutch handle, wind the front crutch adjustment levers to the maximum up position, i.e. in an anti-clockwise direction. (The crutch handle is stowed in a small pouch on the starboard side of the intermediate centre portion of the fuselage.)

(iv). Remove the bomb carriers from inside the bomb cell by releasing the trip levers in the bomb gear housings. This will need one man inside the fuselage to release the lever, and one man in the bomb bay to remove the carrier.

(v). Fit the bomb carrier to the top of the bomb, which should have been wheeled underneath the bomb cell on the ground, and adjust the bomb crutches evenly only sufficient to steady the bomb while it is being raised,

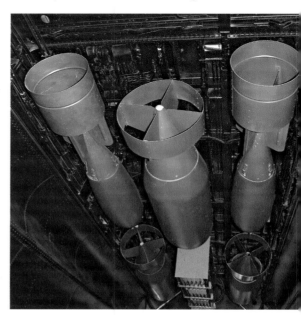

otherwise the carrier may distort and prevent its fitting into the housing.

(vi). Adjust the fuse-setting control link from the fusing box on the carrier to the bomb.

(vii). Set the supporting lever in the bomb gear housing in the cocked position.

(viii). Hold the ratchet on the 'quick-wind-in' side of the bomb winch in the FREE position and pull sufficient length of cable off the drum to pass through the housing.

(ix). Lift the winch reaction pad in the housing so that the winch nose can be fitted after the winch cable has been passed through.

(x). Again hold the ratchet in the FREE position, pull the cable to the ground and carefully fit the ball end to the ball socket on the carrier.

(xi). Take up the free length of the cable on the 'quick-wind-in'.

(xii). After ensuring that the ball end is still engaging the ball socket, proceed to raise the bomb and carrier to the bomb gear housing. The bomb and carrier should be kept in a fore-and-aft position during the lifting operations. (A bomb steadying fork may be used for this purpose.)

(xiii). When the carrier is near the bomb housing, ensure that the guide rollers on the carrier engage the guide in the housing, and the supporting pin engages the support hook. This will force the hook upwards and operate the trip lever which will lock the supporting hook round the pin on the carrier. (The completion of this operation will be indicated by a loud click as the trip lever operates.) Ensure that the locking pawl is fully engaged.

(xiv). Unwind the cable a few turns to ensure that the carrier is locked in the housing.

(xv). The ball end of the cable should then be disengaged from the socket.

(xvi). Tighten the front carrier crutches by winding the crutch handle in a clockwise direction. Tighten the bomb crutches securely, but take care not to over-crutch or the bomb may be 'hung up'.

(xvii). The electrical connection between the plug on the carrier and the socket at the rear of the bomb gear housing, should

then be made and locked, but first ensure that jettison bars on the selector box are at SAFE.

(xviii). After completion of the bomb loading operations, remove the safety brackets from the bomb door jacks, fit the cover plates to the top of the bomb gear housing, and carry out the usual 'light test'.

ABOVE A mixed bomb load, just awaiting a 'Cookie'. *(Jarrod Cotter)*

BELOW To the left of the pilot's seat is the bomb door lever. *(Paul Blackah/Crown Copyright)*

'However great you consider the Lancaster
to be, it must be understood that it will
never be as great as the men who flew it.'
The Panton family,
owners of NX611 *Just Jane*

Chapter Three

The owner's view

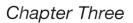

Nowadays the chance of anyone becoming the owner of a Lancaster is very unlikely. There are currently only fifteen complete Lancasters on display around the world, with another under restoration and one stored dismantled. All the owners of these aircraft fully appreciate their heritage and rarity, and the phenomenal price tag that would be attached to one probably isn't the biggest hurdle – it's getting one to be offered for sale in the first place!

LEFT At East Kirkby in Lincolnshire, in the heart of 'Bomber County', Lancaster VII NX611 is kept in fully serviceable taxiable condition at the Lincolnshire Aviation Heritage Centre. Visitors can regularly see a 'Lanc' running in its natural environment here, and get a taste of night 'ops' during World War Two. In this scene from November 2007, a poppy wreath placed in the bomb aimer's blister pays a fitting tribute to the lost crews of Bomber Command as Flight Lieutenant Mike Leckey runs up the Merlins. *(Jarrod Cotter)*

ABOVE One of East Kirkby's many charms is the sight of a Lancaster operating from a grass runway during its scheduled taxi run days – a sight little seen since World War Two.
(Jarrod Cotter)

Purchasing an airworthy Lancaster is hardly likely!

To see even a static Lancaster offered for sale nowadays would be a miracle, so the prospect of an *airworthy* example becoming available is remote! The Lincolnshire Aviation Heritage Centre's NX611 at East Kirkby represents the most recent instance of anyone acquiring a Lancaster in recently airworthy condition, and while nowadays it stays firmly on the ground this aircraft is very much alive.

The museum is a memorial dedicated to all Bomber Command personnel who never returned home from operations, but especially to Pilot Officer Christopher Panton. Christopher was a flight engineer with No 433 Squadron RCAF based at Skipton-on-Swale, Yorkshire, flying the Handley Page Halifax. He was lost on operations over Nuremburg on the night of 30/31 March 1944, aged just 19.

Two of Christopher's bothers, Fred Panton MBE and Harold Panton, were young teenagers still at school when their brother died, and as they grew older they became determined to do something to commemorate his memory. What

transpired is a fascinating story, the fruits of which can be enjoyed by all today.

We pick up Lancaster Mark VII NX611's story in early November 1962, when, numbered WU-15, it made its way to Noumeau, New Caledonia – a French island located about 1,000 miles east of Australia. It was one of three Lancasters employed by the French Navy for a variety of tasks including air-sea rescue and communication duties across a wide region of the Pacific. After just two years all three French Lancs were withdrawn from service.

Around this time the UK-based Historic Aircraft Preservation Society was looking to preserve a Lancaster. The French offered HAPS one of their retiring examples free of charge, and even flew it to Australia for collection. WU-15 arrived at Bankstown, near Sydney, New South Wales, in August 1964.

Prior to its lengthy flight home the Lancaster would need a thorough overhaul. In order to pay for this and the flight back to the UK a fund-raising campaign was put in hand. Assistance came from the Hawker Siddeley Group, the Royal Australian Air Force, the RAF, Shell and QANTAS, as well as many aviation enthusiasts.

WU-15 was overhauled, fitted with an extra fuel tank and test flown. Then, on 23 April 1965, with the British civil registration G-ASXX, it was moved to Mascot near Sydney, ready for its much-publicised departure. It took off on the first leg of the 12,000-mile journey home two days later on 25 April. The trip took nine days and totalled around 70 flying hours, with the aircraft landing at Biggin Hill, Kent, on 13 May.

Due to the expiry of the permitted hours on one engine and propeller, G-ASXX was then grounded. Restoration work to return it to the air took around two years and included the overhaul and re-certification of the engines, propellers and various other systems. It was repainted in a night-time camouflage scheme and regained its original RAF serial number, NX611. It later received the name *Guy Gibson* at a ceremony attended by the famous bomber pilot's father.

On 6 May 1967 NX611 took off for its first test flight. A second was flown the following day, with a third air test being carried out on 9 May. The fourth test flight took place on 17 May and after the rectification of faults encountered on previous sorties this was completely successful.

NX611's first public appearance was set for the weekend of 19/20 May 1967, when the bomber was to travel to RAF Scampton to mark the 24th anniversary of the 'Dam Busters' raid. It made several other appearances, but without the required amount of sponsorship funding the expense of operating it, coupled with the fact that the RAF's PA474 was flying again around the same time, was to lead to NX611 being grounded again. Its last sponsored display took place at Filton, Bristol, on 15 June 1968.

HAPS was soon wound up, and Reflectaire Ltd took over its assets. On 30 March 1969 NX611 set off for its new home at Lavenham, Suffolk. On 7 February 1970 the aircraft was on the move again, this time to Hullavington, Wiltshire. NX611's final flight took place on 26 June 1970, when it set off for Squires Gate, Blackpool, Lancashire. Since its arrival back in the UK NX611 had made a total of 14 flights.

It was planned to establish an aviation museum at Blackpool and to keep the Lancaster in airworthy trim as its centrepiece. However, the closest it came to this was during film work in February 1971 which saw NX611 carry out fast taxi runs along the main runway. This was to be the last time it moved under its own power for almost 25 years. Financial difficulties were later experienced and a receiver was called in.

An auction of the museum's exhibits was held on 29 April 1972. The sales catalogue was given the title 'The Contents of the Aeronautical Museum'. On the header page inside it stated: 'Including an Avro Lancaster Bomber "Guy Gibson."' The catalogue also mentioned that the Lancaster would taxi during the morning.

It was the last lot, No 63. Its description read:

'An Avro Lancaster Bomber with black and beige camouflage, with French Air Force markings; G.L.C. registered NX611; built early 1945, adapted to carry life-boats, later christened *Guy Gibson*.

'This aircraft flew first with the RAF, but not on operations, during the war, was rebuilt in the early 1950s and sold to the French Air Force and flew on operations in French Indo-China and was on supply drops at Dien Bien Phu; acquired by the present vendor in 1965, when it was flown back from Australia to this country.

It has since flown many times, particularly in relation to 617 Squadron of the RAF – The Dam Busters.

'Together with a quantity of spares and parts and the jacks and ignition harness complete.'

Even though an engine was fired up in an attempt to impress potential buyers before the auction began at 2:00pm, surprisingly few bidders came forward and the Lanc failed to reach its reserve of £12,000 – which seems incredible nowadays. In the crowd that day was Fred Panton.

Soon after the auction the Right Honourable Lord Lilford purchased the aircraft privately. It was his desire that the Lancaster should remain in Britain. However, though NX611 had found a new owner its future was not assured. A lengthy spell of exposure to salt air and a general lack of expert maintenance had taken their toll, and during the next winter a rapid deterioration of its overall condition followed, especially to the engines and propellers. Something needed to be done urgently, otherwise the bomber could be in danger of deteriorating severely and subsequently facing the scrapheap.

Fred Panton, who had himself been interested in buying the aircraft, stepped in to persuade the RAF to preserve it. In January 1973 an engineering officer from RAF Scampton inspected the Lanc and concluded that it would be possible to dismantle the bomber, move it to the Lincolnshire base and restore it as a static exhibit. Lord Lilford visited Scampton and agreed to offer it on long-term loan. Dismantling work began in August, when RAF Scampton sent a team up to Blackpool. It took nine days and six Queen Mary trailer-loads to take NX611 apart and transport it to Scampton.

Following a thorough and meticulous restoration, NX611 was positioned at the main gate on 10 April 1974. Final reassembly began the following day and the difficult task of positioning the Lanc was completed on the 25th, when it was finally lowered onto the concrete and steel supports which had been constructed for it. On 17 May Lord Lilford unveiled a plaque and officially handed NX611 over to RAF Scampton's Station Commander, Group Captain J.B. Fitzpatrick. To round off the ceremony, PA474 carried out a flypast over the newly installed gate guard.

BELOW Former BBMF engineer Ian Hickling works on NX611's number 3 engine during its winter maintenance phase. *(Jarrod Cotter)*

As the end of the ten-year loan period agreed by Lord Lilford approached, various parties became interested in buying NX611. Amongst them were Fred and Harold Panton, who had been keen at the time of the Blackpool auction and had also been involved in the negotiations which took it to Scampton. The Lincolnshire farming brothers purchased the Lancaster from Lord Lilford on 1 September 1983. Its future secure, the Lanc remained on gate guard duties at Scampton until May 1988, by which time it had spent almost 14 years there.

The task of dismantling the bomber at RAF Scampton began at around the beginning of April 1988. In order to achieve this it had to be moved onto a newly constructed car parking area opposite the guardroom, in order for there to be a firm hard standing for all the heavy ground equipment, such as trestles, jacks and safety raisers. The first major components to be removed were the outboard engines and all four propeller assemblies. As things progressed the fuselage was split into three sections for the move by road to East Kirkby, a distance of about 30 miles.

Following arrival at its new home, the task of putting the Lancaster back together

began. This took the team from RAF Abingdon approximately four months to complete. Once reassembled NX611 received some cosmetic attention and was given the codes of the former bomber station's two resident Lancaster squadrons, Nos 57 and 630. A 57 Squadron DX-C code was applied on the starboard side and a 630 Squadron LE-C code to port. Fred and Harold's long-held wish to pay tribute to Christopher and all his fellow Bomber Command airmen was now a reality.

In 1993 they decided that the bomber shouldn't remain just a static exhibit. Former RAF engineers Ian Hickling and Roy Jarman were therefore recruited, and in January 1994 they began the task of coaxing the four Rolls-Royce Merlins back to life one by one. Within just three months the number 3 engine (starboard inner) was ready. A first start up was carried out on 20 April – the first time one of the aircraft's engines had been run since the Blackpool auction back in 1972. This was followed by a longer run the next evening, when the site was opened to the public to watch the Lancaster's engine spinning a propeller.

It took just another three months to get the number 2 engine (port inner) going. This was

ABOVE **East Kirkby also boasts a restored World War Two control tower fully fitted out inside, which visitors can look around.**
(Jarrod Cotter)

NX611 moved under its own power for the first time since February 1971.

Number 1 engine (port outer) was the next to be got running, on 6 April 1995. To celebrate NX611's 50th birthday in fine style, it carried out its first public taxi run in front of a large and appreciative crowd on the 22nd of the same month. Number 4 engine (starboard outer) burst into life just under three months later, and on 13 August the Lancaster's first four-engined taxi run was carried out, complete with a flypast courtesy of PA474, which lives just a few miles from East Kirkby.

Since then NX611 has carried out regular taxi runs on scheduled days at the museum. Perhaps the most emotive taxi runs are those at night-time events, when the bomber can be seen firing up its engines at a former Bomber Command base in its natural operational environment of darkness.

While such a sight is impressive enough, on 14 February 2002 another milestone occurred when NX611 performed a tail up fast taxi 'take-off' run on the remainder of East Kirkby's former runway. The wonderful sight of the Lincolnshire Aviation Heritage Centre's Lanc performing these runs was courtesy of a BBC filming contract for a drama entitled *Night Flight*.

This brought the sight of a Lancaster on East Kirkby's runway for the first time since around 1946, as well as being the first time NX611's tailwheel had been lifted into the air under its own power since the 1971 film work at Blackpool. Nowadays the East Kirkby museum site has expanded and includes a grass runway. Daylight taxi runs now take the bomber onto this, providing another evocative and rare sight, of a Lanc running on the grass. Occasionally fast taxi tail-up runs are carried out too.

ABOVE NX611's port side *Just Jane* nose art. *(Jarrod Cotter)*

fired up on 28 July, when the opportunity was also taken to start number 3 and see the two inboard engines running together.

The following autumn and winter were spent overhauling various other systems, including the brakes. So delighted was everyone with their progress that thoughts now turned to getting NX611 into a condition where it would be able to taxi under its own power. By the spring of 1995 the bomber was ready to roll. With both inboards running, on 4 March BBMF Lancaster pilot Flight Lieutenant Mike Chatterton eased the throttles forward and

BELOW Night-time taxi runs by NX611 always attract a large crowd – even on a cold November evening. *(Jarrod Cotter)*

The Canadian viewpoint

Apart from the BBMF's PA474, the Canadian Warplane Heritage Museum's FM213 is the world's only other airworthy Lancaster. The type has such strong links with Canada that it is most fitting that the country boasts its own airworthy Lanc. It is painted to represent Mark X KB726, in which Pilot Officer Andrew Mynarski RCAF carried out a supremely brave act that cost him his life to save another, for which he was posthumously awarded the Victoria Cross.

Here we ask Don Schofield, the Lancaster's training captain, what it means to have the bomber flying in the skies of Canada and how they go about it.

Q: Many RCAF crews flew on Lancasters with Bomber Command. In your experience what does it mean to them and their relatives to have FM213 flying in Canada?

A: To have a living, breathing connection with their past that they can see, hear, and touch is a multi-faceted experience for many of the veterans and their families. For many it fosters fond memories of the camaraderie of their youth and intense pride (and relief) of returning from battles well fought.

For others it is a searing reminder of the pain of the loss of comrades, or equally ugly experiences such as wounds and imprisonment. For those, however, who survived at least relatively unscathed, it is a means to explain to generations two and sometimes three their junior 'what Granddad did in the war'.

I once had the experience of meeting Jack Friday of the original Mynarski crew who was doing just that. Jack flew with us that day and after we landed we went into the canteen, and while we were having post flight tea he took out his logbook and had me enter and sign off the final entry, crossing out the last 'missing' line, and replacing it with 'returned', with the date and time etc.

That says it all better than I ever could.

Q: How does flying the Lancaster compare to other types you have flown in your career, especially more modern multi-pistons?

A: The only similarity between the Lanc and the Airbus 330 on which I did my last flight was that they were both Rolls-Royce powered. I have heard it said that nothing advances technology faster than a war. I was just lucky enough to have started in the pilot business in the late 1950s when we were about to go all jet. I was trained on the Chipmunk and then

Will NX611 ever fly again?

Ever since it was brought back to running order, there has been much debate and speculation about whether or not NX611 will one day be made airworthy. Here the Panton family give their thoughts on what it means to them to have the Lancaster at the Lincolnshire Aviation Heritage Centre, and the latest feelings concerning its future:

'We view our Lancaster NX611 *Just Jane* as being a living memorial and tribute to Bomber Command and all of the men and women who lost their lives operating them. There is never a day goes by when someone around the world does not talk about a Lancaster, and that shows to us its importance in keeping the memory of the Second World War alive.

'Both the sight and sound of the Lancaster are enormously evocative and have different effects on different people. For some it evokes feelings of respect and reverence, for others it symbolises sadness and great loss, and for others it evokes pride and patriotism. But however great you consider the Lancaster to be, it must be understood that it will never be as great as the men who flew them.

'Many people ask us if our Lancaster will fly again. To this question there is currently no definitive answer. There are three factors; the will to do it; the logistics of operating it; and the finances needed to restore it.

'From 1994 to 2007 we have been running the engines and from 1996 to 2007 we have been taxiing, therefore flight is the obvious next step. The aircraft is in excellent condition and it is not beyond the realms of possibility to be able to fly it, after all, that is what they were made to do. There are quite a few static Lancasters in museums that will never be able to fly again, so it seems a great waste not to fly a Lancaster that has the ability to be made airworthy. Flying NX611 *Just Jane* has never been ruled out as a possibility and it has always been considered, but it is not something that has been decided yet. With one Lancaster already flying in Britain, we are in no rush to fly ours.

'There is always ongoing restoration and repairs to *Just Jane* after the taxiing season, throughout the winter period. She is looking in good shape and we hope to keep her that way. We are now trying to build up a good spares store to aid the years of operation that we hope to have with the aircraft. As always we are looking for new displays that we can do, such as tail-up taxi runs. We view the operation of the Lancaster as a way of educating men, women and children about the aircraft and the hardships of the Second World War. We hope to be educating people for many years to come.'

ABOVE FM213 in the skies of Canada, a flying tribute to the many RCAF personnel who flew with Bomber Command.
*(Doug Fisher/
www.warbirddepot.com)*

BELOW Don Schofield in the cockpit of FM213 – the 'Mynarski Memorial Lancaster'.
*(Doug Fisher/
www.warbirddepot.com)*

the Harvard, so tailwheel, prop-driven stuff was not unfamiliar. When I got to the T-33 at AFS my reaction was 'Wow, this is easy!' Other than the basic movement of controls there is no real parity between these generations of aircraft. When we were restoring the Lanc some people commented how it would never get past the modern design criteria. This in no way diminishes the fact that, in its day, the Lanc was 'state of the art.'

Q: Can you give an outline of the procedures you must use to fly the Lancaster around in the restricted airspace of North America, and the principal equipment needed?

A: Procedures and equipment. A very complicated question with an elegantly simple answer – GPS! We have a wonderful GPS on board that allows us to go just about anywhere with ease and precision. We are all active or retired airline types and all very familiar with our operating area, so it is not often a real challenge. One of the more 'different' experiences of late was operating VFR in the New York City area, all of which, by the way, was done with very detailed briefings and blessings of the FAA. Whizzing past, or rather under, the approaches to JFK at 500ft, past the Verazzano Narrows bridge, the Statue of Liberty, and looking down into the hole at Ground Zero was what modern youth would call a 'real mind blowing experience'!

Although we do not as a matter of policy fly in IMC, the GPS I mentioned plus the standard IFR kit of VOR, DME, ADF, LORAN C etc make it pretty hard to get lost. If we are not really familiar we *always* get detailed briefings, often from ATC or from local pilots whenever we operate in a 'new' venue. We always carry the required flight information publications for both VFR and IFR flight and the ATC types are usually so fascinated by the opportunity to control a real World War Two aircraft that they are unfailingly helpful.

Our GPS is a Garmin 296, which is *so* clever that in addition to a moving map it has a complete instrument panel presentation that draws all of its information from listening to the constellation of satellites.

We have all of the required kit to operate IFR (as opposed to IMC) because it gives

us the liberty to transit big metropolitan high-density traffic areas (read: many, many aeroplanes!) with ease and legality. We generally choose not to fly in clouds or rain unless we absolutely have to because, to be frank, she leaks like a sieve! One sage said that flying her in heavy rain would probably require the installation of bilge pumps!

Q: When you fly a crew members' sortie, what's it like flying to Toronto around the CN Tower and over Niagara Falls?

A: Flying around Toronto and Niagara is just a matter of being intimately aware of local procedures, *ie* the Canada Flight Supplement is very specific about flight procedures such as aircraft type, altitudes and speeds, orbit headings, directions of turns, and noise sensitive areas etc. All in the line of good flight safety. The others on board may get to watch the scenery but we are usually quite busy keeping up with what is nowadays called 'situational awareness'.

ABOVE FM213 taxies in after a sortie with Don Schofield in the captain's seat.
(Doug Fisher/ www.warbirddepot.com)

Insurance and running costs

In the post-9/11 world, warbird insurance became a huge cost factor and is growing ever more so. People are becoming concerned that this could effectively halt the operation of some large multi-engined warbirds.

The cost of insurance for a Lancaster is difficult to determine. The BBMF's example is a military owned and operated aircraft, and as such there is no private insurance company providing a policy. The Canadian Lanc is insured under a policy that provides universal liability cover for the CWHM's entire, large fleet of airworthy aircraft. It is not rated separately, and therefore has no policy specifically tailored for it. Besides, to get a quote for a policy you need to know the value of the item to be insured, and the value of an airworthy Lancaster is something nobody seems keen to guess at...

The following short list provides some idea of PA474's running costs at the time of writing:

Oil – approximately £11 per gallon (37 gallons x 4 tanks).
Fuel – approximately £1.20 per litre (average 600 gallons, or about 2,730 litres, loaded per trip).
Tyres – £1,300 each; will last for 150 landings.
Brake bags – £2,000; will last for between 10 and 200 landings.
Mid-upper turret fairing – approximately £45,000.
Flame dampers for exhaust shrouds – £32,000.
Bomb aimer's blister – £4,500.
Overhaul of main undercarriage oleo – approximately £6,500.
Engine overhaul – £80,000 to £110,000.
Cost of a Major service taking 14,858 man hours – £920,528.

‘We are keenly aware that the Lancaster is a priceless piece of national heritage.’

Flight Lieutenant Ed Straw,
Lancaster pilot.

Chapter Four

The crew's view

Where once flying an RAF Lancaster was a nightly task required of many, nowadays it is a privilege experienced by very few. They do not take this for granted, being fully aware of exactly why they are airborne in this flying memorial. The purpose of this chapter is to provide you with an insight into what it is like to fly in the BBMF's Lancaster, from the various crew members' points of view.

LEFT With Flight Lieutenant Ed Straw as captain, this is a rare scene of the crew of PA474 hard at work during a sortie. (Ed Straw)

Pre-flight checks

The external and internal pre-flight checks, as stated in Lancaster technical manual AP2062A-14, are carried out by the engineer, and are as follows:

External pre-flight check

Carry out a systematic inspection, starting at the entrance door and working clockwise around the aircraft. Check for signs of leaks and damage and check that all panels and hatches are in position and fasteners are secure. Ensure that the airframe is clear of snow, ice and hoar frost. Check:

First aid kit	In position
Rear turret	Condition
Tailwheel	Checked
Static vent	Checked, plug removed
Pressure head	Checked, cover removed
VOR aerial	Flag removed
Tyres	Checked, condition noted
External power supply	In position, ON when required

Internal pre-flight check

Ground/flight switch	FLIGHT, check voltage. Set to GROUND when external power available
Intercom switches	NORMAL – emergency
Navigator's radio and master RT switch	ON
Navigator's instruments	Condition. OFF
U/C warning horn	TEST
Air intake control	COLD AIR (wire locked)
Bomb door selector lever	OPEN
Captain's radio	ON
Navigation lights switch	As required
External lights master switch	As required
U/C position indicator	ON. Day/night screens set DAY. 2 greens. Changeover checked
Accelerometer	Reset
Flight instruments	Checked
Direction indicator	Caged
Landing lamps	UP
Boost gauges	Static readings noted
Flap position indicator	Switch ON. Check reading against flap position
Fire warning and feathering button lights	Test. Day/night screens set to DAY
Supercharger switch	M gear
Master cocks	Checked. OFF
Boost control cut-out lever	OFF
Throttles	Full and free movement, set maximum
Pneumatic pressure gauge	Pressure available (minimum 250psi)
Handbrake	ON. Check pressure at each wheel, handbrake OFF
Co-pilot's VHF radio	ON
Radiator shutters	AUTOMATIC
Emergency air selector knob	In (OFF), tell-tale wire locked
Electrical services switch	ON
Engine instruments	Checked
Fuel contents	Checked, agree with F700
Fuel booster pumps	TEST in turn, check ammeter reading (3–5 amps). OFF
Tank selector cocks	Checked. Set as required

Introduction

Despite the maintenance and checks carried out by the ground crew, it is the responsibility of the aircrew to carry out various final checks before each flight to ensure that their aircraft is airworthy. On the Lancaster the majority of the technical checks are carried out by the flight engineer, However, the other members of the crew are responsible for ensuring that their stations are ready for flight.

Start-up

Prior to the starting checks the flight engineer is to ensure that the external power, if available, is ON and the pilot (the captain) is to ensure that the undercarriage locks (4) are removed. In the following checklists
P = pilot (left-hand seat);
C = co-pilot (right-hand seat);
N = navigator;
E = flight engineer;
G = ground crew.

BELOW The flight engineer doing his pre-flight checks. Here Wing Commander Colin Reeves examines the undercarriage. *(Paul Blackah/ Crown Copyright)*

Pre-start checks

F700	P	Signed
Chocks	P/C	In position left and right
Engineer's pre-flight checks	E	Satisfactory and complete. POB ('People on Board')
Flying controls	P	Full and free movement
Brakes	P/C	ON (P), pressure checked (C) (minimum 200psi)
Undercarriage	P	Down and bolted, 2 greens
Flap selector	C	Neutral
Radios	N/C	On and checked
Master cocks	C	OFF
Fuel	E	Number ... tanks selected
Helmets	P	On

Starting checks

Crew intercom	ALL	Checked
Emergency intercom	N	Selected and checked, re-select normal
G4B inverter	N	ON (cxDG) ('check directional gyro')
Static boost	C	Noted
Booster coil master switch	C	ON
Throttles	C	Half-inch open, friction set
RPM levers	C	Maximum friction set
Start clearance	N	Obtained
Anti-collision lights	C	ON
Crew chief's start checks	G	All locks, covers, plug and ladder removed. Fire guard in position. Area clear for start

Engine start-up drill

The following drill should be followed for each engine. The items in italics are stated unchallenged, but monitored by the checklist reader.

Start number 3 engine

Master cock	C	Number 3 ON
Ignition cock	C	Number 3 ON
Clearance	P/G	Clear number 3
		Turning number 3
Fire warning light	C	OUT
Oil pressure	E	*Rising*
rpm	P	*1,100*
Bomb doors	N/G	Closed

(number 3 only)

Start remaining engines in turn

Start number 4
Start number 2
Start number 1

Lancaster start-up

The engine start is usually carried out with two people in the cockpit, one person in each wheel well, standing on the tyre, and one person in front of the Lancaster with a headset, who acts as the safety man. The start-up is carried out following a set procedure, as follows:

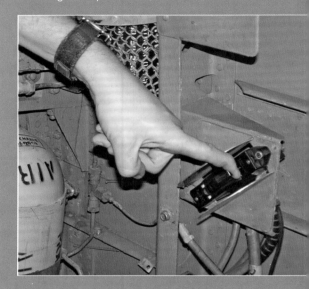

1 Power to the aircraft is switched on by means of the ground flight switch, aft of the forward main spar

2 The control tower is contacted to confirm that the aircraft is about to start engines, and they are informed of the number of personnel on board

3 The undercarriage master switch is set to ON

4 At the same time the instrument panel switch is set to ON

5 The boost coil switch is set to ON

6 The fire system light test is carried out to ensure that the system is working

7 The flap indicator switch is set to ON

8 The brake lever is applied, giving 120psi to the main wheels

9 The lock to the brake lever is put in place; this keeps the brakes on without having to hold the lever

10 The airscrew control is set to FINE

11 The throttle lever on number 3 engine is moved one inch forward

12 The fuel master cock to number 3 engine is set to ON

13 The fuel tank selector cocks are moved to the OUTER TANK position

14 The outer tank fuel pump is set to ON

15 The number 3 engine magneto switch is set to ON

16 The person in the undercarriage bay unscrews the priming pump

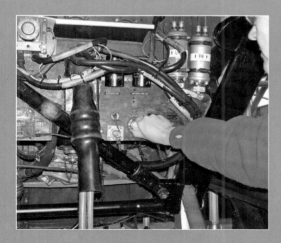

The other engines follow the same procedure from stage 10 on.

17 He then operates the pump 8 to 12 times to prime the engine

18 The switch guard is lifted, the number 3 engine start button is pressed and the engine starts

Once all four engines have started and are up to their correct operating temperatures and pressures, the chocks are removed and the pilot then carries out engine power checks to ensure each engine's magnetos are operating correctly. During this check each engine's rpm is allowed to drop a maximum of 50. If it drops any more than this the aircraft is shut down and the fault is rectified. If the engines are within limits the aircraft then taxies to the runway.

Take-off

After taxiing to the end of the runway, the aircraft lines up for take-off and the following checks are carried out:

Take-off checks

Take-off clearance	N	Obtained
Pressure head heater	E	ON
Radiator shutter	C	Automatic
Windows and hatches	P/C/E	Closed left (P), closed right (C), hatches secure (E)
IFF	N	ON

After these checks have been successfully completed the pilot will begin the run. When the aircraft reaches 90 knots it will become airborne, the undercarriage will be raised, and the following checks are carried out:

After take-off checks

Brakes	P	On, off
Undercarriage	P/E	UP, lights out
Climb power	C	Set
Engine temps and pressures	E	Checked
Flaps	C	UP, indicating selector neutral
Door	E/G	Closed and locked (locked only if leaving the circuit)

Handling pre-display checks

Radios	N/C	Frequency set
Altimeters	P/N	QFE set. Compared
Crew security	ALL	Checked secure
Fuel	E	Checked and set (number ... tanks selected, 1 and 2 booster pumps ON)
Display brief	P	Complete
Anti-collision lights	C	Off

Display flying a Lancaster

BBMF Lancaster Captain Flight Lieutenant Ed Straw gives an insight into a typical display sortie:

Taxiing

'The pre-taxi checks are completed and once the oil temperature on each of the Merlins has reached 40° the aircraft is ready to move. As part of these checks I throttle back the two inboard engines and the ground crew remove the chocks from the main wheels. Once taxi clearance has been obtained, and the crew have re-checked everything is clear of the aircraft, I release the brakes using the lever on the left-hand side of my control column.

'Once taxi speed is reached I call "thousand inboard" and the co-pilot sets 1,000rpm on both inboard engines. I then retard the outboard engines to idle rpm, thus preventing the aircraft from accelerating too much. Taxiing the Lancaster isn't difficult but takes time and practice to feel totally comfortable.

'The pneumatic braking system is basic

and the technique required to taxi is to use a combination of brakes and bursts of engine power. If the rudder pedals are positioned centrally when the brake lever is applied then equal braking will be applied to both main wheels and the aircraft should decelerate in a straight line. By applying left rudder pedal and re-applying the brakes, more braking will be applied on the left side and the aircraft will commence a turn to the left. The same principle applies for the right side, which is called differential braking.

BELOW Taxiing out to
the runway.
(Jarrod Cotter)

ABOVE Flight
Lieutenant Les Munro
was a pilot on the
famous 'Dam Busters'
raid of 16/17 May 1943.
(Courtesy Les Munro)

Les Munro –
'Dam Buster' pilot

The following questions were put to Flight
Lieutenant Les Munro CNZM DSO QSO DFC,
who was one of the pilots on the famous 617
Squadron dams raid of 16/17 May 1943. Les
continued to fly throughout World War Two and
today lives in his native New Zealand.

Q: How did the Lancaster compare with earlier
bomber types you flew, such as the Wellington,
and what do you remember thinking after your
first flight in one?

A: The only other bomber that I flew was the
Wellington and that was at 29 Operational
Training Unit. Bear in mind that it was a twin-
engined plane and I have been asked to
compare it with the four-engined Lancaster
– quite a difference! Both planes, however, had
no vices and were relatively easy to fly. With
the Lanc you were conscious of its extra size
and weight, but you were also conscious that
you had four powerful engines. I was quite
comfortable piloting both planes. I just accepted

the experience of my first flight in a Lanc at
1654 Heavy Conversion Unit as another step in
my flying career.

Q: When fully laden with a heavy bomb
load, how did it cope with take-off and flying
to targets?

A: The Lancaster never had any trouble taking
off with a full bomb load. You were, of course,
governed by the maximum permitted all-up
weight, *ie* the total of the weight of the plane
plus sufficient petrol to make the return trip
to the target and back, plus the bomb load.
The shorter the distance to the target the less
petrol needed and the greater the bomb load;
conversely the longer the distance to the target
the more petrol put in the tanks and the lighter
the bomb load. I seem to remember that when
I first started operations the all-up permitted
weight was 65 or 66,000lb, and as the planes
were fitted with more powerful Merlins this
increased to 72,000lb, probably more by the
end of the war. A further major factor was the
length of the runway to be used and the wind
strength. On a short runway the permitted all-up

weight was reduced to provide a safety margin. Invariably, however, the long runway was used for most operational take-offs.

Q: How well could it withstand hits by flak and machine gun fire?

A: Unlike the Wellington, with its geodetic construction and consequent ability to withstand quite a lot of damage, the Lanc was more vulnerable. It could, however, withstand quite a bit of damage if it was not subjected to a direct hit or did not catch fire.

Q: Did you ever return to base with one or more engines hit and shut down, and if so what do you remember of how the Lancaster coped?

A: On one occasion I had an engine failure just after take-off and it is testimony to the power of the Merlins that I was able to continue to the target at St Etienne with a full bomb load on three motors, arriving shortly after the rest of the squadron, and when the attack was aborted returned to base with the bomb load still on board. On two other occasions I had an engine put out of action but was able to return to base without any problem.

Q: What was it like to be the captain of your crew and aircraft, and how much did you feel the burden of responsibility for their safety?

A: I believe that I assumed the responsibility of the captaincy of aircraft and crew without any problems. The responsibility for their safety was just part of the job as pilot that I accepted without thinking of it as a major issue. By the same token other crew members such as the navigator and the gunners had equal responsibility for the safety of the aircraft and crew on an operation: the navigator by ensuring that we didn't stray over heavily defended areas on the way to and from the target, and the gunners by searching the sky for night-fighters.

Q: How would you feel physically and mentally after a particularly long-distance sortie, to Berlin for example?

A: On a long trip I had no problems mentally as far as I am aware – check with my crew in the hereafter to confirm that! I think that it was only natural that you would arrive back after, say, an eight- or nine-hour trip feeling somewhat jaded, but I never reached the stage that I had difficulty in maintaining alertness.

BELOW The Lancaster BIII (Special) that dominates this photo was being flown by Les Munro.
(Courtesy Les Munro)

ABOVE Wing
Commander Guy
Penrose Gibson,
the most famous
Lancaster pilot and
leader of 617 Squadron
on the 'Dam Busters'
raid. *(RAF Museum)*

ABOVE RIGHT The
Victoria Cross is
Britain's highest
award for gallantry
and was earned by
ten Lancaster aircrew.
(Jarrod Cotter)

Wing Commander Guy Gibson VC DSO and Bar DFC and Bar

The most famous Lancaster pilot of all was Wing Commander Guy Penrose Gibson, who formed and led No 617 Squadron on the 'Dam Busters' raid of 16/17 May 1943. After having dropped the 'bouncing bomb' from his Lancaster (ED932 AJ-G) over the Möhne Dam in Germany, Gibson stayed at the target and accompanied his fellow pilots during their runs in order to draw the enemy's fire. This allowed the other pilots to concentrate on the demanding task of releasing their special weapons successfully – at just 60ft above the water and within the precise distance at which they had to be released. He then led the remainder of his squadron to the Eder Dam, where with further disregard for his own safety he repeated his tactics and once again drew the enemy's fire so that the attack would succeed. For his actions that night Gibson was awarded the Victoria Cross. He was killed on 17 September the following year while flying a Mosquito, having insisted on staying on operations when his superiors had wanted him not to.

In all, ten Lancaster aircrew were awarded the Victoria Cross during World War Two. In chronological order, the recipients were: Squadron Leader John Nettleton (17 April 1942); Wing Commander Guy Gibson (16/17 May 1943); Flight Lieutenant William Reid (3 December 1943); Sergeant Norman Jackson (26 April 1944); Pilot Officer Andrew Mynarski (12 June 1944); Squadron Leader Ian Bazalgette (4 August 1944); Wing Commander Leonard Cheshire (8 September 1944); Squadron Leader Robert Palmer (23 December 1944); Flight Sergeant George Thompson (1 January 1945); and Captain Edwin Swales (23 February 1945).

'Once the aircraft is turning, opposite brake is required to stop the turn and point the aircraft in the required direction. The aircraft has considerable momentum in the turn, and opposite brake needs to be applied with some anticipation in order to stop the turn at the desired heading. However, once confidence has been gained using the brakes it's helpful to make use of the outboard engines. For example, if you want to turn to the right a burst of number 1 engine will start the aircraft turning, and – with the appropriate anticipation – a burst from number 4 engine will stop the turn. The advantage of using the outboard engines instead of the brakes is that no system brake pressure is expended.

'The Lancaster is taxied using a combination of these techniques. Throughout the taxi, the system brake pressure is continually monitored on the triple pneumatic brake gauge on the right-hand side of the cockpit, to ensure that the pressure is adequate. Fully charged system pressure is 450psi and the minimum pressure for taxi is 200psi. Small compressors on three of the four engines help replenish the system.'

Take-off

'Having taxied onto the runway I line the aircraft up with the nose pointing to the right of the centreline, so that I'm looking to the left of the nose along the line of the runway. Once all the pre-take-off checks are complete, I call "Zero boost" and the co-pilot advances the throttles until zero boost is indicated on the gauges.

'Holding the aircraft on the brakes, with it straining to move, I re-check the engine instruments before looking at each engine. If all is well I release my grip on the brake lever, allowing the aircraft to start moving. I anticipate the swing to the left with right rudder and may even use some right brake to keep the aircraft straight.

ABOVE Captain and co-pilot on hold awaiting clearance to move onto the active runway. *(Ed Straw)*

ABOVE During the take-off run the tail-wheel is raised off the ground very quickly to adopt the correct attitude for rotation. *(Jarrod Cotter)*

'On take-off the Lancaster has a marked swing to port which has to be countered immediately if directional control is to be maintained. This swing is more pronounced if the surface wind is from the left because, being a tail dragger, the aircraft will want to "weathercock" into wind. If the wind is from the right this helps me to control the swing. Once satisfied that the rolling line is good, and anticipating more swing with power applied, I call for "Plus 7".

'The co-pilot advances the throttles evenly and the noise level rises dramatically as the Merlins come alive. I counter the further swing to the left with increasing amounts of right rudder, while keeping the control column fully back to keep the tailwheel on the ground. It's not uncommon to use all available right rudder on take-off, and in the early stages of the run some right brake may also be required to keep the aircraft straight.

'As the speed increases the situation quickly improves, as the greater airflow over the rudders means they become more effective. Once I sense the increased rudder authority I push forward on the column to raise the tail and gain the take-off attitude. As the tail rises the rudders come directly into line with the propeller slipstream, providing even more rudder authority, and the need for right rudder is considerably reduced.

'Throughout the take-off I'm looking straight down the runway, using the rudders to remain on the centreline, and aileron to keep the wings level. The co-pilot, holding the throttles in position, is monitoring the engine boost and rpm gauges while the navigator calls the indicated airspeed. At 90 knots [103mph] he calls "Rotate" and I pull back on the control column and select a very shallow climb angle. Once airborne I squeeze the brake lever on to stop the wheels rotating, then off, and call "Gear up". The flight engineer selects the gear lever to the up position and I see the two red lights illuminated to my left side to signify the gear is travelling.

'I maintain the shallow climb angle in order to accelerate the aircraft more quickly and therefore be better placed should we suffer an engine failure. I wait for the two undercarriage lights to go out, signifying the wheels are up, and then re-check the airspeed and altimeter.

Once we have 120 knots [138mph] and 150ft indicated, I call "Flaps up". When the co-pilot selects the flap lever to up there's a pronounced nose drop with the Lancaster. I anticipate this by pulling back on the control column to maintain the attitude.

'With the aircraft now accelerating through 130 knots [150mph] I call for "Plus 4, 24", meaning I want plus 4 boost and 2,400rpm – the Lancaster's normal climb power setting. Achieving the required setting isn't as straightforward as it may seem, and it takes some getting used to. The throttles are moved first and brought back to plus 4 boost. Then the rpm levers are lowered to reduce the engine rpm.

'The co-pilot will set the approximate rpm before accurately setting the inboard engines using the rpm gauges. He'll then synchronise each outboard engine by looking through the already set inboard prop, adjusting the outboard prop until it stops moving in relation to the inboard propeller. He then repeats this for the other engine. With the co-pilot selecting climb power, I call for the "After take-off and climb checks", which the navigator will call out from his checklist. Meanwhile, I have climbed the aircraft at 140 knots [161mph] to 500 or perhaps 1,000ft and levelled off. Once 150 knots [172mph] airspeed is indicated, I call "Zero 1900" – zero boost and 1,900rpm – and the co-pilot will repeat the process for this new setting. This power setting results in an indicated airspeed of 150 knots, our normal cruise speed, with a fuel consumption of approximately 150 gallons per hour.'

Display

'Displaying the Lancaster is extremely rewarding and in many ways easy. By "easy", I mean that being such an iconic aircraft the Lancaster does all the hard work of impressing the crowd for me. I have no need to perform energetic manoeuvres or adopt extreme attitudes, nor would I want to.

'We know the public want to see, hear, and feel the magic of the aircraft and we can

BELOW The first pass of the Lancaster display is carried out in 'clean' configuration. *(Jarrod Cotter)*

achieve all that with the gentle manoeuvres we perform throughout the display. We are keenly aware that the Lancaster is a priceless piece of national heritage, and my responsibility as pilot is to display it gently and safely and not subject the airframe to unnecessary fatigue.

'The classic sight of the BBMF is as a three-ship formation, the Lancaster leading with a Spitfire and Hurricane on either wing. Running into the display venue I line up and fly the aircraft along the display line at 300ft and approximately 160 knots [184mph]. As we reach the end of the display line, or at an appropriate point, the navigator will call "Fighters, break break go". On the word "Go" the fighters break away, and once clear I manoeuvre the Lancaster to hold position behind the crowd at 500ft.

'The first fighter will commence his display, lasting approximately 4 minutes 30 seconds;

ABOVE View over Flight Lieutenant Ed Straw's shoulder as the Lancaster flies over Duxford's runway. *(Crown Copyright)*

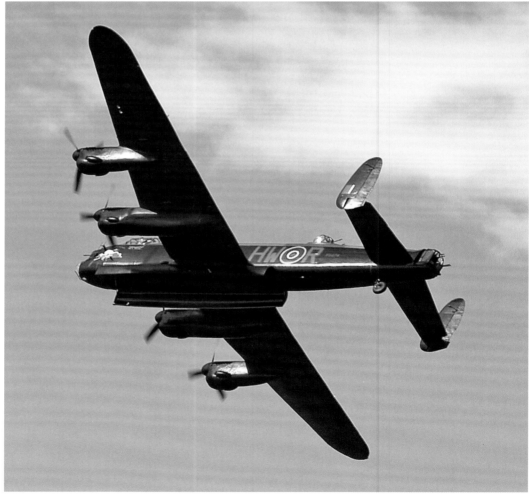

RIGHT Pass with bomb bay doors open. *(Jarrod Cotter)*

the second fighter display will be shorter at approximately 3 minutes and 30 seconds. We receive "1 minute" and "30 seconds to go" calls from the fighters and I use these cues to accurately position the bomber for the take-over. The final pass of the second fighter is at 100ft along the display line, pulling up into a victory roll. The Lancaster should be running in to take over as soon as this victory roll is complete.

'When we receive the "1 minute" call I instruct the co-pilot to increase the engine rpm to 2,400 and re-confirm that all the pre-display checks are complete. These checks ensure that the aircraft is correctly configured to safely carry out a display. I commence my first run at 100ft and 160 knots for a "clean" pass along the display line, allowing the watching crowd to absorb the magnificent sight and sound of the Lancaster.

'The navigator will call display datum and start his stopwatch, calling the time in seconds beyond the datum. At an appropriate time beyond the datum, based on the wind and length of crowd line, I initiate a climbing turn to 500ft and bank the aircraft away from the crowd in order to return the Bomber to "crowd centre". Once the climb is commenced I call "Minus 4" (minus 4 boost) and as soon as the airspeed reduces below 150 knots call "Bomb doors open".

'The bomb door lever is by my left side but, because I have both hands on the control column throughout the display, the navigator behind me has to lean forward and operate the doors. I see the amber light illuminate in front of me, signifying the doors are opening, and call "Zero boost" to stabilise the airspeed at approximately 140 knots. I continue turning the aircraft back towards the display datum and

ABOVE A wheels-
down pass is another
aspect of the bomber's
display sequence.
(Jarrod Cotter)

descend to 300ft and fly in front of the crowd
with 30° to 40° angle of bank, allowing them a
good view of the bomb bay.

'From "crowd centre" I continue this turn
through 360°. Any turn in the Lancaster requires
the pilot to "lead" with a good deal of rudder,
as well as using aileron, and throughout this
turn I often need to make large control inputs,
particularly in aileron, to maintain the desired
turn. With the bomb doors open I also need to
maintain the airspeed below 150 knots.

'Halfway around the 360° turn I have climbed
to 400ft and call "Bomb doors closed", and
the navigator operates the lever. I continue the
turn, checking the bomb door light goes out to

confirm the doors are shut, and complete the
turn with a second pass through display datum
at 300ft, tracking away at 45° to the display
line in a gentle climb. I check again that the
airspeed is below 150 knots and call "Below
150, flaps 20".

'The co-pilot will move his left hand from
the throttles to the flap lever on his left side
and push the lever down whilst looking at the
flap gauge on his right side. Once the flap
indicator gauge shows 20° he returns the flap
lever to neutral and both hands go back on
the throttles.

'Having re-checked the airspeed I call
"Below 150, gear down" and the flight engineer

the airspeed and call for the appropriate boost setting, normally zero boost, to maintain 120 knots. Now on the display line approaching crowd centre, I squeeze the brake lever on, then off, to stop any wheel rotation, and call "Gear up". The flight engineer moves the undercarriage lever to the "up" position and my two green indicator lights turn red.

'Next, just before display datum, I call "Plus 7", the co-pilot pushes the throttles forward and we experience the fantastic noise and surge of the four Rolls-Royce Merlin engines. I bank the aircraft away from the crowd and aim to track out at 45° to the display line, climbing to 500ft. With the surge of engine power the aircraft tries to pitch nose-up, so as well as turning I am pushing forward on the control column. I wait until we accelerate through 120 knots and call "Flaps up", the co-pilot obliging. At this stage the two fighter aircraft are closing in on the bomber to re-join on the wing, so my flying needs to be as smooth as possible as I position the Lancaster for the final pass. I maintain plus 7 boost and 2,850rpm until 140 knots is achieved and call "Plus 4, 24' (plus 4 boost, 2,400rpm).

'The airspeed is important here because the fighter on the inside of the turn will be slower than the bomber. For the fighters, particularly in close formation, any airspeed below 140 knots is slow and very uncomfortable, so, as the formation leader, I must ensure our airspeed is in excess of 140 knots and preferably above 150.

'The final pass along the display line is at 300ft in three-ship formation. Descending from 500ft in the turn I call for "Plus 2" or "Zero boost" to maintain airspeed in excess of 150 knots while keeping at 2,400rpm. If the formation intends to land at the venue the final pass will be planned in the direction of the in-use runway, so that at the end of the crowd line the navigator can call "Fighters, break break go", whereupon they can initiate their break to land.

'The Lancaster will continue up-wind to allow sufficient space from the fighters ahead before turning downwind at 500ft to land. The entire BBMF three-ship display is given a 15-minute slot by display planners, while the Lancaster display alone takes approximately five minutes.

lowers the undercarriage lever situated between the seats and the undercarriage starts to move. I am made aware of this by the noise of the wheels lowering and by the two red lights appearing on the left-hand side of my instrument panel. I commence a gentle turn back towards the crowd, checking that I have two green lights to indicate that the undercarriage is down, and position the aircraft to fly down the display line at 100ft in the "approach" configuration.

'Approaching the display line in a gentle descent at 120 knots I call "2850" and the co-pilot raises the rpm levers, increasing the engine rpm from 2,400 to 2,850. I continue to monitor

'Finally, it's worth mentioning just how busy the rest of the crew are throughout the entire Lancaster display. The navigator and flight engineer aren't only selecting the services as described, but are helping with lookout, positioning, and clearing turns, as well as fulfilling their individual tasks. The flight engineer monitors his panel, checking the health of each engine and managing the fuel, while the navigator operates the radios, as well as making preparations for the next venue. The co-pilot is kept extremely busy, continuously adjusting the throttle and rpm levers and synchronising the engines. Finally, all three have the very important task of monitoring my performance, checking that my actions are correct and safe, and offering support if required. Displaying the Lancaster is a team effort.'

Circuit and landing

'The Lancaster circuit is flown at 500ft and is most appropriately called a "Bomber Circuit". When on the downwind leg I confirm 2,400rpm and zero boost is set, then check that the airspeed is below 150 knots and call "Below 150, gear down". The flight engineer lowers the undercarriage lever and I hear the noise of the wheels travelling and see the two red indicator lights illuminated. I wait 20 to 25 seconds for the two lights to go green, indicating the wheels are down, and call "Below 150, flaps 20".

'The co-pilot lowers the flap lever until the flap gauge shows 20° and then returns the lever to neutral. With flap I have to move the control column forward to maintain the attitude and re-trim in pitch.

'I then request the pre-landing checks, which are challenge and response checks initiated by the navigator. He calls "Undercarriage". I check that the undercarriage lever is down and that the safety bolt is over the top of the lever, and re-check that I have two greens indicating the wheels are locked down. I respond "Down, bolted, two greens".

'Next he calls "Brakes". I check the brake lever is off and call "Off". The co-pilot looks at

the triple brake pressure gauge situated on the right side of the cockpit and checks that there is good system pressure with no pressure at the wheels. He calls "Good pressure, zero at the wheels".

'The navigator then calls "Rpm". The co-pilot checks the rpm is 2,400 and calls "2400". Then the navigator calls "Flap", and the co-pilot checks the flap gauge and lever and calls "Flaps 20, indicator neutral". After this the navigator calls "Pre-landing checks complete".

'I extend the downwind leg of the circuit until the runway threshold is behind the trailing edge of the wing before turning "finals". There's no need to turn early, as the best approach is a long shallow one – a steep approach is not recommended.

'I call "Flap 40". The co-pilot lowers the flap lever to 40° while I push the control column forward to maintain attitude and initiate the turn. The navigator then calls "Lancaster finals, gear down", and once established in the turn I call "2850", the co-pilot raising all four rpm levers to

increase engine rpm to 2,850. My airspeed is 125 knots.

'At this stage I re-check the boost gauges, as often the boost has dropped off a little, and the co-pilot resets zero boost. The navigator calls out the final approach checks, which confirms that landing clearance has been obtained, the flap is at 40° and rpm is 2,850. I am aiming to reduce the airspeed to 90 knots [103mph] over the threshold and ideally want 105 knots [120mph] half-way around the turn. On the approach I will call for "Minus 2", "Minus 4", and "Minus 6" to reduce the airspeed, looking to be at minus 6 and 90 knots just above the touchdown point.

'Due to weather no two days are exactly the same, so the point at which I ask the co-pilot for these power reductions will vary. I fly a shallow approach, working hard to remain exactly on the centreline, and in the final stages use a "wing down" technique to deal with any crosswinds. At approximately 200ft I change from tracking the aircraft down the centreline to pointing the

BELOW The final pass is another 'clean' flypast. *(Jarrod Cotter)*

PA474 flight test schedule

Current aircraft limitations and restrictions are not to be exceeded.

GENERAL DATA

Pilot . . . .
Co-Pilot. . . . .
Engineer . . . .
Navigator . . . .
Basic Weight . . . .
Fuel Weight . . . .
Aircrew Weight . . . .
Other Load . . . .
Take-off AUW . . . .

CERTIFICATE OF AIRWORTHINESS

Certified that this aircraft has been flight tested in accordance with the appropriate Flight Test Schedule and that it is:

*a. Airworthy and functionally serviceable to the required standard.

*b. Airworthy and functionally serviceable subject to minor rectification as entered in F700 and does not require further tests.

*c. To be retested after rectification as entered in the F700.

Signed . . . .
Name . . . .
Rank . . . .
Date . . . .
*Delete as applicable.

AIRCRAFT GENERAL

Ambient Air Temperature . . . .
QFE . . . .
Pneumatic Pressure . . . .
Brake Pressure Port . . . .
Brake Pressure Stb . . . .
Emergency Air Pressure
   (1,100 to 1,200 lb/in) . . . .
Hydraulic Accumulator Pressure
   (220 lb/in) . . . .
Voltage . . . .

Fuel Contents	No.1 Port	. . . .
	No.2 Port	. . . .
	No.3 Port	. . . .
	No.1 Stb	. . . .
	No.2 Stb	. . . .
	No.3 Stb	. . . .

Controls and Trims –
Check full, free & correct sense.   satis/unsatis

AFTER START

After starting No.3 –
   Close Bomb Doors   satis/unsatis

At 1,200 RPM	No.1	No.2	No.3	No.4
Oil pressure (Min 30psi)	. . . .	. . . .	. . . .	. . . .
Oil Temperature (Min 15°c)	. . . .	. . . .	. . . .	. . . .
Rad Temperature (Min 40°c)	. . . .	. . . .	. . . .	. . . .
Fuel Pressure Warning Light	on/out	on/out	on/out	on/out
Magneto Dead Cut	yes/no	yes/no	yes/no	yes/no
Generator Charge (1,300rpm)			. . . .	. . . .
Vacuum			. . . .	. . . .
Voltage			. . . . volts	

TAXIING

Check operation of:

Compass, Remote	satis/unsatis
Magnetic	satis/unsatis
DI	satis/unsatis
Turn & Slip	satis/unsatis

Maximum Brake Pressure at each wheel   Port . . . . psi
                                             Stb . . . . psi

Function of Brakes, judder and fade,
Captain's Port satis/unsatis Remarks . . . .
          Stb satis/unsatis Remarks . . . .
Co-Pilot's Port satis/unsatis Remarks . . . .
          Stb satis/unsatis Remarks . . . .

PRE-TAKEOFF

At Zero Boost	No.1	No.2	No.3	No.4
RPM	. . . .	. . . .	. . . .	. . . .
Oil Pressure (min 30psi)	. . . .	. . . .	. . . .	. . . .
Oil Temperature (min 15°c)	. . . .	. . . .	. . . .	. . . .
Rad Temperature (min 60°c)	. . . .	. . . .	. . . .	. . . .
Mag Drop Port (max 150)	. . . .	. . . .	. . . .	. . . .
Mag Drop Stbd (max 150)	. . . .	. . . .	. . . .	. . . .
Supercharger Operation	yes/no	yes/no	yes/no	yes/no
Generator Charge	. . . . amps		. . . . amps	

TAKE-OFF

Start timing at zero boost and brakes off.
Open throttles to +7 boost.
Unstick at . . . . knots IAS
Climb at 140 kts. With +4 boost and
2400 rpm to 7000ft if possible.

Time to 3,000ft	. . . . min	. . . . sec
Time to 5,000ft	. . . . min	. . . . sec
Time to 7,000ft	. . . . min	. . . . sec

CRUISING

At 3,000ft, fly at 150 kts and 2,000rpm.

In steady conditions	No.1	No.2	No.3	No.4
Boost	....	....	....	....
Oil Pressure	....	....	....	....
Oil Temperature (max 90°c)	....	....	....	....
Rad Temperature(max 150°c)	....	....	....	....
Supercharger Operation	yes/no	yes/no	yes/no	yes/no
Generator Charge			....	....

Voltage .... volts

Hydraulic Accumulator Pressure (600–1,000psi) .... psi

Trim: Elevator Trim .... Div Nose up/down/neutral
      Rudder Trim .... Div Port/Starboard/neutral
      Aileron Trim .... Div Port/Starboard/neutral

STALLING

Aircraft clean, Pitch fully fine, Throttle closed

Stalling speed (onset of buffet) .... Kts
Stalling speed (full stall) .... Kts
Wing Drop Port/Starboard/neutral
Undercarriage and flaps lowered .... Kts
Wing Drop Port/Starboard/neutral

OPERATION OF UNDERCARRIAGE AND FLAPS.

At 150kts straight and level time the following:

Undercarriage down .... secs
Flaps Down .... secs
Flaps Up .... secs
Undercarriage up .... secs
Bomb doors open .... secs
Bomb doors shut .... secs

ENGINES

At 2,000ft, 150kts and 2,000rpm:

	No.1	No.2	No.3	No.4
Boost	....	....	....	....
Oil Pressure	....	....	....	....
Rad Temperature	....	....	....	....
Feathering	yes/no	yes/no	yes/no	yes/no
Unfeathering	yes/no	yes/no	yes/no	yes/no
Generators	.... amps		.... amps	

Remarks ....
....
....
....
....

LANDING/SHUT DOWN

After landing, at 1,200rpm:	No.1	No.2	No.3	No.4
Oil Pressure	....	....	....	....
Oil Temperature	....	....	....	....
Rad Temperature (max 100°)	....	....	....	....

After shutting down engines 1, 3 and 4.

Operate flaps fully down then fully up   Satis/Unsatis

Fuel Contents   No.1   port ....   Galls used ....
                No.2   port ....   Galls used ....
                No.3   port ....   Galls used ....
                No.1   stbd ....   Galls used ....
                No.2   stbd ....   Galls used ....
                No.3   stbd ....   Galls used ....

Total flight time ....   Total fuel used ....

INSTRUMENTS

Check each instrument for function:

Compass   satis/unsatis
DI   satis/unsatis
A H   satis/unsatis
T&S   satis/unsatis
Altimeter   satis/unsatis
RCDI   satis/unsatis
ASI   satis/unsatis

RADIO

UHF   satis/unsatis
VHF   satis/unsatis

GENERAL REMARKS

....
....
....
....
....
....
....
....

RIGHT Time for the captain to take the Lancaster home to Coningsby.
(Crown Copyright)

nose directly at the runway and preventing any drift by banking the aircraft into the wind, hence the term "wing down technique". To prevent the

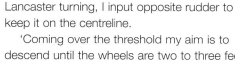

RIGHT Flight Lieutenant Ed Straw signs the aircraft in.
(Crown Copyright)

Lancaster turning, I input opposite rudder to keep it on the centreline.

'Coming over the threshold my aim is to descend until the wheels are two to three feet above the runway and level off momentarily. I re-check I have the Bomber absolutely straight before calling "Cut". The co-pilot gently retards the throttles while I prevent any nose drop by pulling back on the control column while looking straight down the runway. The main wheels should touch gently down on the runway, whereupon I call "Flap up" in order to take the lift from the wings and transfer the weight of the aircraft to the wheels. It is very important to keep the aircraft straight at this point and I do this using rudder, while keeping the wings level with ailerons.

'Once the aircraft is settled on the main wheels and decelerating I gently pull back on the column to lower the tailwheel. If necessary I'll apply some brake and complete the landing run. Once we've decelerated to taxi speed I call for the after landing checks.'

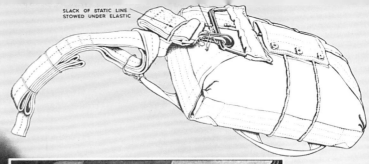

SLACK OF STATIC LINE
STOWED UNDER ELASTIC

, fly air-craft at 130 A.S.I.
flaps down.

ounded man to bomb
ompartment and place him
acing aft.

ounded man's parachute
Fit parachute. Remove

Static Line from stowage
on starboard side of front
it. Care should be taken
threads keeping the Static
ded up are not broken.
ap-hook at end of Static
attach to parachute as

5. Pass the safety becket on the Static Line through the double 8-cord safety loop; then pass the small snap-hook through the safety becket.

6. Snap the hook down on to the rip-cord handle. Insert and close the safety pin to lock the shroud of the snap-hook.

7. Stow the slack of the Static Line, between the becket and the snap-hook, under the adjacent pack elastic to obviate all danger of this slack length fouling a protuberance during evacuation and thus causing premature release.

8. Open and jettison front escape hatch.

9. Slide the man through the exit, feet first, facing aft. Care must be taken to keep his hands to his sides. Do not hold on to the Static Line.

RIP CORD RING
SNAP HOOK
SAFETY PIN
STATIC LINE
PACK CARRYING HANDLE
STATIC LINE SAFETY BECKET   DOUBLE 8-CORD SAFETY LOOP

ANCASTER I II III & X – *Parachute Drill (With Static Line)*

AIR DIAGRAM 3011
SHEET Nº 2 / Nº OF SHEETS 2
OCT. 1943

PREPARED BY MINISTRY OF AIRCRAFT PRODUCTION FOR PROMULGATION BY **AIR MINISTRY**

FOR H.M. STATIONERY OFFICE BY FLEMINGS, LEICESTER. 51-4352

(RAF Museum)

Emergency equipment and controls

Technical manual *AP2062A Volume I* provides the following details regarding the emergency equipment carried aboard a Lancaster during the Second World War:

Fire extinguishers – The automatic fire extinguishers mounted one in each nacelle may also be operated by the pilot from push-buttons on the right of the instrument panel. Six hand fire extinguishers are provided, of which one for the pilot is mounted on the port cockpit rail.

Parachute and crash exits – Parachute exits may be made from the hatch in the floor of the nose or from the main entrance door. The pilot's parachute is stowed immediately behind his seat on a panel at the end of the navigator's table. The hatch in the nose is released by means of the handle at the centre, lifted inwards and jettisoned through the hole. Three 'push-out' type emergency exits are fitted in the roof of the fuselage, one in the canopy above the pilot, one just forward of the rear spar, and one above the rear end of the main floor. These should not be used as parachute exits.

Dinghy – A Type J dinghy stowed in the starboard [main]plane may be inflated and released in any of three ways:

(i). By pulling the release cord running inside the fuselage along the roof aft of the rear spar.

(ii). From outside by means of the loop on the starboard side adjacent to the leading edge of the tail plane.

(iii). Automatically by an immersion switch. A special emergency pack is supplied with the aircraft; it is carried in the dinghy compartment stowed on top of the dinghy to which it is attached by means of a lanyard. In addition to this pack, standard emergency packs Type 4 and Type 7 are stowed on the starboard side of the fuselage, just aft of the rear spar.

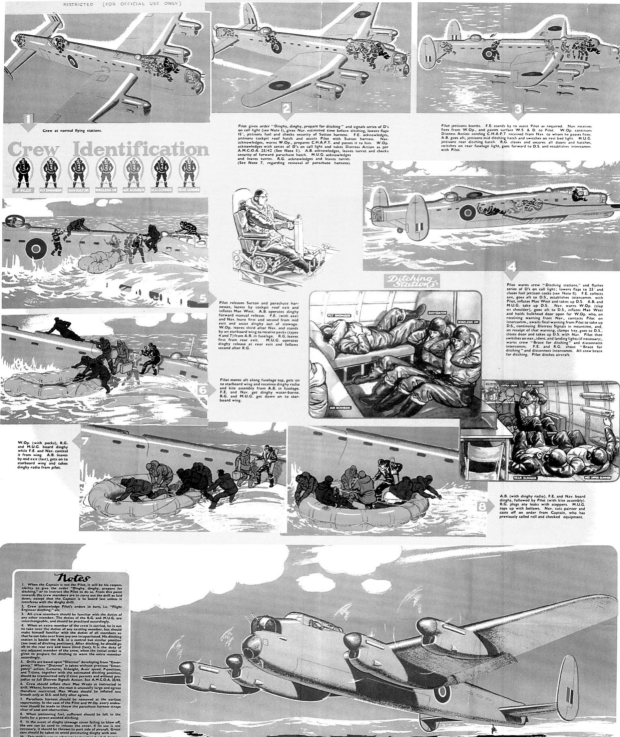

(RAF Museum)

LEFT Entrance to the rear gun turret, showing the gunner's parachute stowage position. *(Paul Blackah/ Crown Copyright)*

Crash axe and first-aid outfit – These items are stowed on the starboard side aft of the entrance door.

Fuel jettisoning – The contents of both No.1 fuel tanks may be jettisoned by lifting and turning anti-clockwise the hydraulic control handle on the left of the pilot's seat. The flaps should be lowered 15 degrees and speed reduced to 150 mph IAS before jettisoning.

FAR LEFT First-aid outfit, stowed on the starboard side aft of the entrance door and accessed by pulling the handle. *(Jarrod Cotter)*

LEFT Emergency equipment at the rear spar, including fire-axe and gloves. *(Paul Blackah/ Crown Copyright)*

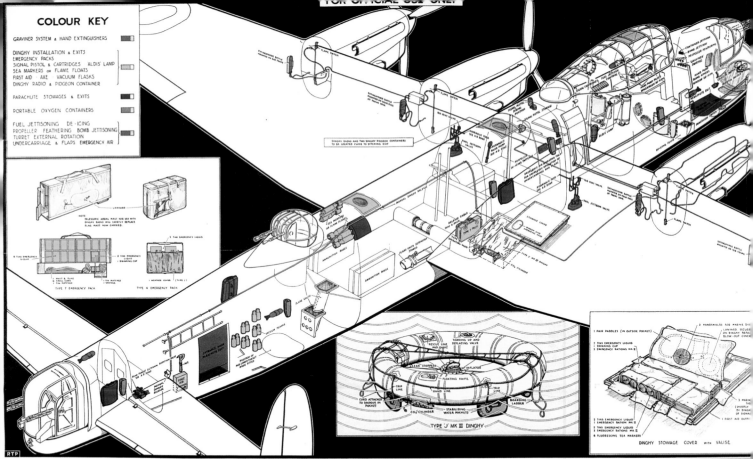

COLOUR KEY

GRAVINER SYSTEM & HAND EXTINGUISHERS

DINGHY INSTALLATION & EXITS
EMERGENCY PACKS
SIGNAL PISTOL & CARTRIDGES   ALDIS' LAMP
SEA MARKERS or FLAME FLOATS
FIRST AID   AXE   VACUUM FLASKS
DINGHY RADIO & PIDGEON CONTAINER

PARACHUTE STOWAGES & EXITS

PORTABLE OXYGEN CONTAINERS

FUEL JETTISONING   DE-ICING
PROPELLER FEATHERING   BOMB JETTISONING
TURRET EXTERNAL ROTATION
UNDERCARRIAGE & FLAPS EMERGENCY AIR

EMERGENCY EQUIPMENT & EXITS – LANCASTER I

AIR DIAGRAM 2062

AIR MINISTRY
PREPARED BY
MINISTRY OF AIRCRAFT PRODUCTION

(RAF Museum)

If the flaps will not lower by the hydraulic system, do not attempt to lower them by the compressed air system, as this will also cause the undercarriage to lower.

Bomb jettisoning – The complete bomb load (excluding bomb containers) may be jettisoned after the bomb doors have been opened, by means of the jettison handle fitted on the right side of the instrument panel; if bomb containers are carried they should be jettisoned first by the bomb container jettison switch fitted to the left of the bomb jettison handle.

RIGHT There are three 'push-out' emergency exits fitted in the roof of the fuselage, this being the one in the canopy above the pilot. These should not be used as parachute exits.
(Jarrod Cotter)

Navigating the Lancaster

BBMF Navigation Leader Squadron Leader Jeff Hesketh profiles the role of the 'Nav':

'As navigators know, preparation is all-important in the outcome of a sortie, flypast or display. To this end, for each upcoming season the flypast and display bids are collated by the previous October; a rough outline plan is then proposed by New Year and firmed up by March. Sorties range from annual fixtures such as Biggin Hill and Duxford, where we "land away", to others varying from local to national importance or remembrance.

'The Lancaster is only allocated 100 flying hours during the display season, to preserve fatigue on the airframe. However, 110 hours are actually planned, knowing that some hours will be lost due to inclement weather and also aircraft unserviceability. These hours also have to include pilot and navigator training, display work-up and Public Display Authorisation flights. Initial event timing is completed by the BBMF Adjutant, who does an outstanding job in keeping tabs on every detail of administration.

'To minimise flight time, the initial timing plan is based on a straight line from Coningsby to the display/flypast venue flown at 150 knots (keeps the mental maths easy – 2½nm per minute), together with a timing four-minute hold at the IP or "initials point" – a distinctive feature of vertical or horizontal extent, *eg* a mast, road junction, forest shape or lake – if it's a "timed" flypast such as a Royal event or graduation revue. More details are put on the plan by the navigator, who draws up charts on ¼ mil or ½ mil maps, with an OS 1:50K map used for the "IP to target" run.

'These charts are further embellished with the radio frequencies required, timings, tracks and distances, together with potential diversion airfield details. For a display we always plan to "run in" in the direction we wish to "run out", to achieve minimum flying time to the next event. Quite often two routes are planned where a transit is required over high ground, one "straight line" for good weather and a bad-weather option taking a longer lower route – for example, Coningsby to Blackpool has a "straight line" route over the Pennines to the

ABOVE Squadron Leader Jeff Hesketh is the BBMF's Navigation Leader.
(Crown Copyright)

North of Manchester Control Zone for good weather, while we have a back-up route flying through the Crewe to Wigan corridor in case of bad weather over the hills – and still make the venues on time!

'We try to avoid flying through the "chain link fences" of controlled airspace, but many times it's unavoidable and requires co-ordination by the navigator with the ATC unit involved. Almost without exception we're allowed into their controlled airspace. We plan to avoid glider sites and light airfields, used predominantly at the weekends and Bank Holidays, not to mention the danger areas, firing ranges and restricted airspace that increasingly cover the UK.

'If we are in radio contact with airfields as we transit from venue to venue and the ATC request a fly-through, then providing it does not interfere with our timing we are more than happy to oblige – cleared down to 100ft and 300ft. The Lancaster flying on its own is planned to fly at 1,000ft utilising the low-level flying system. This is to avoid the increasingly busy general aviation traffic above. It's quite entertaining when a private Cessna tries to fly near the Lancaster, perhaps blissfully unaware of our "fighter escort" 2,000ft above! At Nav School we were always taught to avoid large towns, but with this aircraft it's appreciated if we fly over. The Lancaster attracts no noise complaints, only comments such as can we come back again and *lower*!

'Many of our trips are what we call "out and back", where the Lancaster takes off from Coningsby for, typically, five flypast locations (three passes each) and two display locations (each five minutes), and then returns to base. This example equates to seven events for one aircraft on one day. The flight time for this is typically 70 minutes.

'These types of sortie save our ground engineers time travelling to turn the aircraft and, in addition, should we happen to go u/s it would be at Coningsby. In the 2007 display season more than 700 individual aircraft appearances were made from an

initially planned 573 events, which comprised some 110 displays and 463 flypasts – not a bad achievement for volunteer aircrew, and a testament to the dedicated maintenance undertaken by our 27 engineers.

'Due to the distinctive sound of the four Merlins and our slow speed compared with modern-day jet fighters, many observers on the ground soon become aware of our presence. On many transits, cricket matches are stopped; golfers wave and housewives are seen waving tea towels dashing into their gardens; cars stop ahead and their occupants stand and wave. A far cry from World War Two.

'Flying down to 250ft, which is our minimum height outside airfields and over England's green and pleasant land, it is a very proud feeling indeed. In the Lancaster, the navigator stands behind the pilot, map and stopwatch in hand, using his "Mk 1 eyeballs" to view over the pilot's shoulder or look out of the blister to the side – back to basics indeed. To aid us we sometimes

BELOW Approaching RAF Wyton for the sunset ceremony as described in the text, with the white water tower (visible to the right of the canopy) used as a reference point. *(Paul Powell/ Crown Copyright)*

use a stand-alone Garmin 496 in the Lancaster, to act as secondary aid to map and stopwatch and to give an accurate groundspeed display.

'The navigator is responsible for the R/T, using the radio, with callsign "Lancaster", and using the IFF, which is located on the Nav table behind. In summer it can get very hot in the cockpit, with the canopy acting like a greenhouse. Low-level flying requires fix points with vertical extent – masts, chimneys and so on – but above 1,500 feet we can use lakes, forest shapes and towns, so our flying is a blend of the two. Basically we navigate with a heading and time for that navigation leg, working from big feature to little feature for our tracking, slowly inching or "walking" our fingers over our prepared maps, which have been folded to achieve maximum effect and fit our nav bag – when you see the crew walk out to the Lancaster the navigator is easily identified by his distinctive nav bag.

'We describe the next turning point to help the pilots find it, and this is crosschecked against our timing at the turn as to whether we are early or late. Often it is the nav's hand pointing "over there" that steers the way, but all crews work together in the best interests of crew resource management! At first it's all too easy to follow roads and look just in front, but soon you get to find masts minutes ahead so you can settle down to timing checks and maybe admire the view.

'The Lancaster is only allowed to fly VFR (visual flight rules) and not in the dark – that calls for interesting planning where a sunset ceremony at Shrivenham (near Swindon) is required, so as to return east to Coningsby and still land before dark. Very strong emotions are felt by the crew at this time, under the Perspex canopy; as the engine exhaust stubs glow red the thought goes through our minds that it would have been this time of night that the actual bombing raids would have taken off in the war – with many crews sadly not returning.

BELOW A final banked pass shows a delighted group of veterans enjoying the sight and sound of the Lancaster.
(Paul Powell/ Crown Copyright)

'Flying the Lancaster in formation with the Spitfire and Hurricane we use the collective call sign "Memorial Flight". Here planning is slightly different – we don't plan to fly over large towns, as the fighters have a gliding range of 1.5 miles per 1,000 feet should their single engine fail. The Lancaster still flies at 1,000 feet but the fighters will be above in the block, anything from 3,000 to 4,000 feet. I'm told by the fighter pilots that occasionally the Lancaster can be lost from sight – not only due to their poor downward visibility, but because the camouflage works as well today as it did in 1945!

'A further consideration is that when in formation we have to avoid any precipitation as this could cause the fighters' wooden propellers to delaminate, whereas the Lancaster's are metal. In addition, we have to be aware of diversion airfields, which must have a supply of AVGAS for the fighters.

'The Lancaster's speed range in formation is limited; if we're early, we can't fly too slowly because of the fighters – typically below 130 knots – and if we're late we can't accelerate as fast as they can – max 200 knots. Often the Lancaster and fighters separate after one event and fly independently to displays and flypasts, then form up at a nominated time and rendezvous for a three-ship formation display at a major venue before making a night stop away from home base.

'In 2006 I was privileged to navigate the Lancaster for the Queen's 80th Birthday Flypast in June. This was only one part of the day's events – albeit a major one. Flying from Coningsby with four fighters, our first event was a photo shoot en route to a flypast at Waterbeach, followed by a hold at Fairlop for the flypast at Buckingham Palace.

'The Lancaster was to lead the flypast of 49 aircraft of 15 different types, one of the largest formations of aircraft seen over London since World War Two. "Memorial Flight" was our call sign for the Lancaster leading two Spitfires and two Hurricanes, with "Windsor Formation" running in from Clacton at much greater speeds one minute behind.

'The timing was perfect – too early and Her Majesty would not have been on the balcony, and too late and I would have had 44 fast jets coming in close behind me at 280 knots at one minute spacing! An immediate right turn on top of the palace put the Memorial Flight over Lords Cricket ground. Play was stopped for several minutes – what a sight and sound – leather on willow and eight Rolls Royce Merlin engines passing 800ft overhead. Routing over the RAF Museum to the north clearing London Zone, we then passed south-east over the Queen Elizabeth II Bridge to Margate with a Spitfire and Hurricane for a formation display, and finally landed at Manston.

'Other flypasts aren't as grand as that: often they're memorial cairns built of stone, perhaps at the edge of a forest or at a road junction, as a memorial to a downed crew, with just a handful of people in attendance, but nevertheless still as deserving and carried out with the same professionalism. If the visibility is on limits and we are looking out for a group of people accurate navigation and timing is vital, as we don't want to commence a series of flypasts at a nearby car boot sale! Limits are 3.7km, 700ft cloud base for transit, 5km and 1,000ft for displays.

'On the day of a sortie the crew attend a meteorological briefing two hours prior to take-off, and this can often call for a rapid re-plan! The knock-on effect requires new ETA's for the display organisers, and flypast events to be passed or confirmed. Some are cancelled due to the weather in some areas being below our limits. A new plan is then calculated. NOTAMS (Notices to airmen) are checked, indicating that the flight will be active within a radius of two miles around the venue and up to 2,000ft altitude 15 minutes either side of the display time – professionally we strive to be on time.

'A crew briefing by the captain is given one hour before take-off, covering sortie overview, timings, weather, fuel, performance, check-in frequencies and "loser plans" (in case one aircraft drops out). The navigator briefs the route, safety altitudes, diversions, Royal flights, and the all-important time check, together with wind, frequencies to use, times, orientation of the venue and crowd lines at the display or flypast venue. The display by the Lancaster can involve either a "tail chase" or "head-on" take-over from the fighters – this may vary at each display during the sortie.

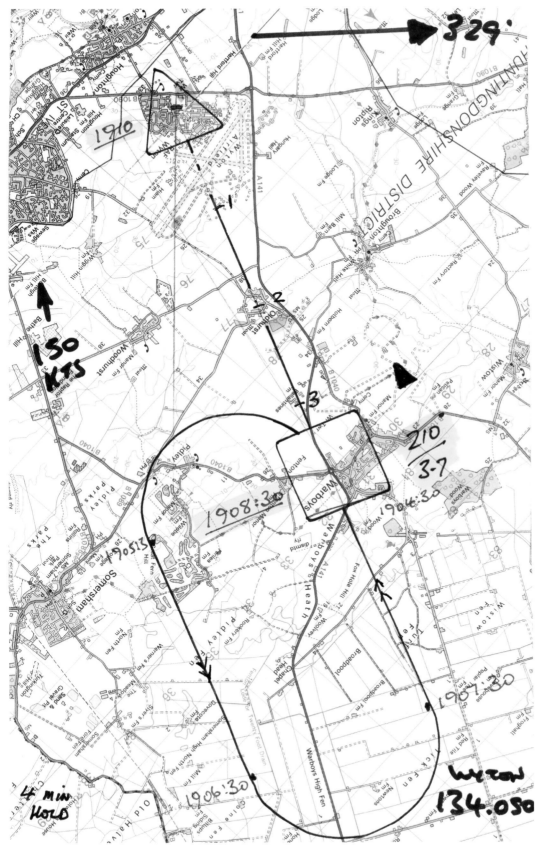

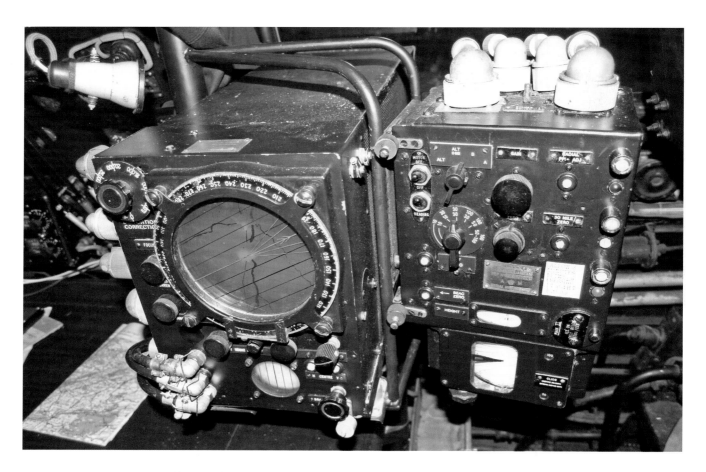

ABOVE Navigator's H2S equipment. This was a ground search mapping radar system used as a fixing aid or for blind marking, introduced in 1942. There were severe restrictions on its use in order to reduce transmissions on which enemy night-fighters could home. A fix was given as bearing and distance from an identified ground feature on the plan position indicator (PPI). The operator's skill in reconciling the PPI display with standard topographical maps was the key to accurate marking or flare dropping. *(Jarrod Cotter)*

'At 35 minutes to go an "out brief" is completed by the captain. With the correct legal authorisation completed, the crew board at 30 minutes before take-off. The engines start at 15 minutes, and run-ups on the mighty Merlin engines are followed by a timed take-off to make the flypast precisely on time and to preserve flying hours on the Lancaster. It's the culmination of weeks of planning, faxes, telephone calls and e-mails to ensure that the aircraft is exactly where it was planned to be and at precisely the required time.

'The map shows a route from RAF Coningsby to RAF Wyton on the occasion of an evening flypast for the Battle of Britain Reception attended by several veteran "Pathfinders". RAF Wyton was the home of the Pathfinders, which in 1945 had seven Lancaster and eleven Mosquito squadrons, located in the vicinity at Wyton, Easington, Gravely and Warboys. The map shows the latest take-off time – corrected for wind (18:50L – the flight always works in local time) to meet the time on target (TOT – 19:10).

'Initial air traffic control is with Coningsby departures, which is studded on a pre-set frequency on the radio behind the navigator. Take-off is completed using the Coningsby QFE setting on the altimeter – transit height 500ft. Once clear of the military air traffic zone the regional Barnsley setting is set, and once clear of Coningsby radio communication is next with Cottesmore, requesting traffic information (flight information service). Routing is then to the west of Crowland glider site to a turning point north of Peterborough, denoted by a railway line crossing a lake.

'At this turning point a timing check will be made and the speed adjusted, together with a change of radio frequency to Peterborough Conington, with the navigator asking for any traffic information. Next leg is onto a track of 158° – corrected for drift to the IP (avoiding Upwood glider site), to a roundabout to the east of Warboys. During this leg the regional pressure setting on the altimeter will be changed to the Chatham regional pressure setting.

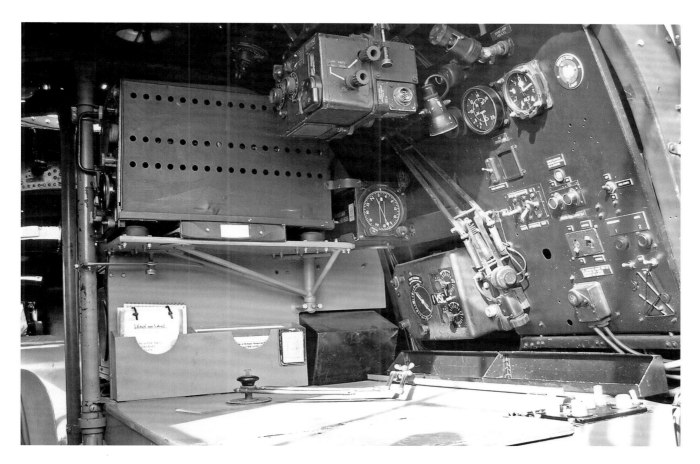

ABOVE Navigator's
station on board
PA474. (Paul Blackah/
Crown Copyright)

'Maps are then changed to the more detailed Ordnance Survey (p.123), which shows the run-in track (210° magnetic) and the time the Lancaster has to leave the IP (19:08.30) at a pre-planned still air groundspeed of 150 knots to make the TOT (19:10). During the transit or during the hold the navigator will fine tune the leaving time corrected for local head or tail winds.

'If the Lancaster is two minutes or more early at the IP, a hold will be carried out. If less than two minutes, then a timing dog-leg will be carried out to make the TOT. Once the aircraft has left the IP a tracking check feature is the wood at just over two miles to run. Looking ahead just to the right of the flypast venue is a large white water tower, and the Lancaster is aligned with this to the right (see photograph p.120).

'As the aircraft approaches within approximately 1½ miles the individual building is identified and the Lancaster is lined up perfectly by the pilot to overfly the Officers' Mess at precisely 19:10, to coincide with the RAF ensign reaching the bottom of the flag pole in front of the Officers' Mess. Three passes are completed, then the return to Coningsby via the escape heading shown (329°) is to the west of Peterborough and Bourne. (See photo of the Wyton Mess p.121.)

'All five of the BBMF's navigators are volunteers. Four are from Cranwell – two Qualified Navigation Instructors teaching advanced fast-jet techniques, and two Central Flying School navigator examiners – while I'm the Standard Evaluation navigator on the E-3D AWACS part of the ISTAR wing at RAF Waddington. The job of a BBMF navigator requires a great deal of commitment, not just from ourselves but from our families as well, as virtually every other weekend between April and October is given up to flying the Flight's Lancaster or Dakota.

'The BBMF is kept going by the passion and selfless commitment shown by all the aircrew, ground crew and support crew. It is indeed an honour and privilege to fly this magnificent aircraft built in May 1945, part of our nation's aviation heritage.'

ABOVE Flight engineer Squadron Leader Ian Morton monitors the various systems on board PA474. *(Crown Copyright)*

The flight engineer's duties

Squadron Leader Ian Morton gives an overview of the flight engineer's duties on board the Lancaster:

'The flight engineer or FE, more commonly known as "Eng" by the crew in today's Royal Air Force, is probably one of the least known members of aircrew. The majority of flight engineers are senior non-commissioned officers who have completed previous service in the RAF as a technician. The remainder are direct entrants, *ie* they joined the service purely to become an FE.

'There are also a small number of FEs who have been commissioned from the ranks to become FE officers, and it is from this small and dwindling branch that the Lancaster FEs are drawn. Very few of them have piston engine experience (the Shackleton retired in 1991) and some have very limited knowledge of propeller theory or practice. With the bare minimum of tuition, each FE selected for the Flight has to study intensively to acquire the technical

knowledge demanded to operate the Lancaster systems safely, using documentation dating back to the 1940s.

'To put things in perspective, although antiquated and very different from today's aircraft the Lancaster systems are straightforward to learn. BBMF's Lancaster is dual-controlled so is operated with two pilots, which means that some of the tasks that originally fell to the FE – the handling of all engine controls including the throttles and RPM levers, along with the flaps – are now the remit of the co-pilot. As a result, after dealing with his routine tasks the FE has plenty of capacity left to devote to the big picture and airmanship. The benefits of having a crewmember in this situation during display flying can't be underestimated.

'Moreover, the FE has always been devoted to the technicalities of his aircraft, and there have been many occasions in the past where this has proved his worth. Take, for example, Flight Sergeant Ben Bennett, who flew in the *Phantom of the Ruhr*, where his knowledge of the Lancaster's flying controls along with his brave acts on ops one night in September 1943 resulted in the award of the Distinguished Flying Medal. It is the memory of FEs like Ben that makes holding the position of FE on the BBMF's Lancaster so rewarding.

'Today's Lancaster FE will visit the BBMF prior to the day of his flying duties to self-brief the sortie. He will ascertain the display venues and read the display files to familiarise himself with the sortie profile and whether the Lancaster is going solo or being accompanied by the Flight's fighters. Having ascertained the total number in the team for the event (the Lancaster will normally carry up to five ground crew in addition to its four flight deck crew), rations are ordered if required.

'The fuel load is checked, the standard usage being 150 gallons per hour, plus 25 gallons for each display and a minimum overhead destination fuel of 280 gallons. He'll also collect the appropriate aeronautical documentation for the route. If landing away from Coningsby he'll crosscheck the airfield's facilities, including handling agent and fuel availability (large holdings of AVGAS and a means of delivering them to the Lancaster are becoming fewer), and will take a copy of any hotel bookings made.

'On the day of the sortie, the Eng will meet with the rest of the crew in the Met office two hours before take-off for the weather briefing, to see what pleasures or challenges lie ahead. Very hot (high 20s) days, strong headwinds or particularly poor weather may result in a last minute increase to the fuel load. On arrival at the Flight he'll meet the Crew Chief and scrutinise the Lancaster's technical log (Form 700) to see that all is in order – the Lancaster rarely flies with acceptable defects but it's vital the crew knows its technical status.

The Eng will then commence his preflight inspection in accordance with his flight reference cards (FRCs), double-checking that the aircraft is serviceable and all systems are set correctly. Once that's done he'll leave the aircraft "Power and Fuel Off", returning to the Flight to complete his weight and balance calculations, attend a crew briefing and a have a welcome cup of tea.

'At 30 minutes prior to take-off the crew will walk to the aircraft and commence the Starting Engines checklist. Whilst the navigator reads the checks, the Eng will respond where required and crosscheck the pilot's and navigator's responses and their actions. The Eng makes checks of the engines' oil pressures and temperatures along with the coolant temperatures during start; before opening up the mighty Merlins, minimum values of these parameters are required.

'Once the engines have been started, the Eng switches the electrics to flight mode and external power is disconnected. He'll then check the fuel flow to ensure a positive flow is available from all tanks under gravity and booster pump supply. During the engine run-up checks oil pressure is monitored and generator outputs checked, and the performance of the magnetos is recorded along with the reference rpm, which is the measure of the power output (the health of the engine). Between engine start and take-off many checks are completed, the

LEFT Flight engineer's panel.
(Crown Copyright)

1 Engine oil pressure gauges
2 Oil temperature gauges
3 Coolant temperature gauges
4 Fuel tank gauges
5 Fuel tank selectors
6 Fuel pump switches (number 3 tanks have guards fitted; they are last tanks selected for use)
7 Low pressure fuel warning light
8 Fuel pump test ammeter
9 Pressure head heater switch
10 Dimmer switch and light
11 Power switch to panel
12 Inspection lamp socket
13 Emergency air selector knob

Eng normally being the crew member with the opportunity to ensure all is in order, from crosschecking the brake pressure to ensuring that no puddles of oil or coolant are left behind on the tarmac after the engine runs.

'With all the checks complete and take-off clearance obtained, the Eng monitors the engines both inside the aircraft and outside as take-off power is applied: 7 inches of boost at 3,000rpm is normally all that's required to pull the old girl safely into the air. Once airborne, on the captain's command the Eng will select undercarriage UP, monitor it travelling, and ensure that the undercarriage doors close – there's no hydraulic contents or pressure gauge, only an hydraulic accumulator gauge which is situated by the crew rest-bunk, well out of sight.

'Once safely flying the power is reduced and the after take-off checks completed. At cruising height, normally 1,000 to 1,500ft, the Eng checks all systems are functioning correctly inside and visually checks the exterior of the aircraft (the occasional venting of coolant occurs on hot days, but oil leaks are very rare indeed).

'During the cruise, the pilots split the flying and engine handling between them and the Nav is busy navigating and making radio calls, which leaves the Eng to be Jack-Of-All-Trades and make sure that all is in order. At some stage he'll record a full set of engine readings to be entered into the F700 on landing, for monitoring engine health. Four pairs of eyes (not to mention the ground crew's) are essential on fine summer days, when the skies above England are busy with light aircraft, gliders, helicopters and other aeronautical machines, so keeping a good lookout is part of everyone's routine.

'During the flight the Eng will initially feed fuel from the inboard tanks (number 1 tanks), to aid wing relief and thus reduce structural fatigue, changing to the outer tanks (numbers 2 and 3) later in the sortie. Switching from number 1 tank to number 2 tank involves going through the OFF position for both engines on that side, so this action is carried out with the utmost care, one wing at a time!

BELOW View from the rear gun turret as Hurricane II PZ865 follows the Lancaster during a transit flight. *(RAF Coningsby/ Crown Copyright)*

'When arriving at the venue most eyes are on the lookout, but having descended to low level (100ft is the absolute minimum) the Eng monitors the engines more closely, especially at the higher power settings. Height and speed are every aviator's friend, so both assume an extra significance during the event.

'The pilots complete the display sequence from memory; however, a rare prompt from "the back" can be welcome. During the display, the Eng will mentally record the engine oil pressure at the higher power settings for entry into the F700 after landing. When the BBMF's fighters accompany the Lancaster, a watchful eye is cast in their direction, both for co-ordination and their well-being.

'Once the display is complete the Eng will make an accurate fuel check and pass the captain a bottle of water from the cold box – he's earned it!

'It's rare that the Lancaster flies in marginal weather conditions but if it's necessary the Eng will help obtain updated weather for the destination and diversion on the aircraft's second radio. Approaching the destination, more checks are completed: the Eng ensures the fuel system is set for landing, lowers the undercarriage, and crosschecks the brake pressures and flap positions along with monitoring the engines.

'After landing the engines are "run up" again, to check their serviceability. This can often cause a delay in proceedings at busy airfields whilst the Lancaster finds a spot to turn into wind and be clear well behind, so that the prop wash doesn't cause any damage.

'Once the engines have been shut down and the fuel and electrics switched off, all that remains is to complete the F700 paperwork and discuss any technical problems with the crew chief. Then, more often than not, there'll be one of the most important aspects of being a crewmember on the BBMF: escorting visitors into and around the aircraft. Accompanying guests around the grand old lady, especially when they're aircrew who flew during World War Two, makes the flight engineer's position, like the rest of the crew, something very special.'

BELOW Looking aft from the astrodome as PA474 banks to starboard. *(Crown Copyright)*

'Patching and replacing parts would mean a long toil, and many were the times we worked day and night without a break.'

Stan Wells,
groundcrew, 626 Squadron

Chapter Five

The engineer's view

It's a great privilege and a big responsibility to care for one of the only two remaining airworthy Lancasters in the world. Personnel who've never worked on historic aircraft soon learn those rare skills that were second nature to engineers and ground crew working on Lancasters during World War Two.

LEFT Ground crew performing an engine change on Lancaster I W4783 *G-for-George* of No 460 Squadron, Royal Australian Air Force, circa May 1943. The work was obviously a success, as this Lanc went on to complete 90 operations before flying to Australia for a War Bond tour. It is now on display in the Australian War Memorial, Canberra. *(RAF Museum)*

ABOVE PA474 awaits
the BBMF engineers
to start work. Note
the mobile tool chest
in the foreground.
The raised platform
around the number 4
engine is purpose-built
for working on the
Lancaster.
(Jarrod Cotter)

While articles about flying on operations are, by their very nature, more interesting, if you ask any wartime Lancaster aircrew member about the contribution of their ground crew they'll always say the same thing: 'It was critical.'

Safety first!

Any aircraft should be treated with respect, especially one that has four propellers! Even when the Lancaster is static you should treat the propellers as 'live'. Prior to moving a propeller a fellow crew member in the cockpit should confirm to you that the magneto switches are in the OFF position, or the engine could fire.

When starting the aircraft care should be taken to ensure that no unauthorised personnel are close to the aircraft, as a propeller blade can easily remove a head. The height of the Lancaster is a safety issue too, and care must

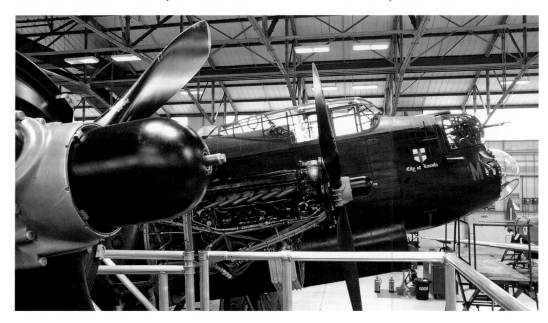

RIGHT With the
spinners removed the
propellers take on a
different look.
(Jarrod Cotter)

be taken when working on the wings, fuselage and tailplane.

Standard safety equipment such as sturdy boots, ear defenders, gloves and overalls are essential to protect against spillage, noise damage, slipping and injury.

When replenishing oils and greases care should be taken to ensure that what you're using is the right product for the job, or mechanical damage can result. Checking is essential, as many containers are similar in appearance.

Finally, before entering the aircraft all your pockets should be emptied, to prevent 'foreign object damage' (FOD).

Tools and working facilities

A good set of BA and BSF spanners and sockets is essential, as is a good general purpose tool kit including screwdrivers, locking pliers and wire cutters. Specialist tools, such as box and peg spanners for stripping components and rigging boards for setting up flying controls, are also required. These can't be easily acquired, but they can be manufactured from original drawings. The size of hangar required is determined by the size and height of the Lancaster, but remember that adequate space must be available to split the aircraft if

necessary, to lift out the turrets, or to remove and refit the engines.

A pair of hydraulic rigs is essential to carry out flap and undercarriage functions, wheel chariots to allow easy removal of the aircraft's main wheels, and engine staging to allow work to be carried out whilst the engines are in place.

Jacking and airframe support

To jack the Lancaster you require two 25-tonne jacks with jacking adaptors (which fit into special sockets that are bolted to the front spar prior to jacking), a tail trestle, a nose trestle and a pair of wing trestles.

In order to raise the aircraft you firstly lift the rear fuselage using a crane, which attaches to an eyebolt screwed into the top rear fuselage. The tail trestle is then put into place at former 33 and the rear fuselage is lowered onto it. The jacks are positioned inboard of the number 2 and 3 engines and the aircraft raised high enough to allow the undercarriage to retract. Then the nose trestle is positioned at former E. Wing trestles are then put into position to steady the aircraft and allow personnel to work on the wings.

A smaller tail trestle can be used for removing the tailwheel. The aircraft must be chocked before raising the tail.

ABOVE Supported by jacks, this is the Lancaster undergoing scheduled annual maintenance during the winter. *(Jarrod Cotter)*

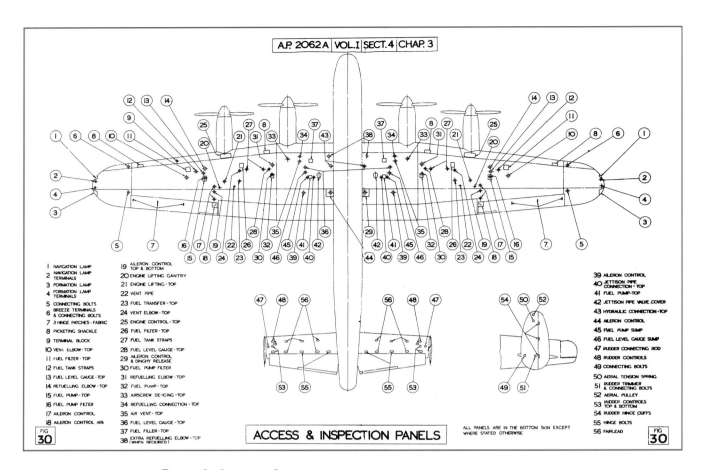

1 NAVIGATION LAMP	19 AILERON CONTROL TOP & BOTTOM	39 AILERON CONTROL
2 NAVIGATION LAMP TERMINALS	20 ENGINE LIFTING GANTRY	40 JETTISON PIPE CONNECTION - TOP
3 FORMATION LAMP	21 ENGINE LIFTING - TOP	41 FUEL PUMP - TOP
4 FORMATION LAMP TERMINALS	22 VENT PIPE	42 JETTISON PIPE VALVE COVER
5 CONNECTING BOLTS	23 FUEL TRANSFER - TOP	43 HYDRAULIC CONNECTION - TOP
6 BREEZE TERMINALS & CONNECTING BOLTS	24 VENT ELBOW - TOP	44 AILERON CONTROL
7 3 HINGE PATCHES - FABRIC	25 ENGINE CONTROL - TOP	45 FUEL PUMP SUMP
8 PICKETING SHACKLE	26 FUEL FILTER - TOP	46 FUEL LEVEL GAUGE SUMP
9 TERMINAL BLOCK	27 FUEL TANK STRAPS	47 RUDDER CONNECTING ROD
10 VENT ELBOW - TOP	28 FUEL LEVEL GAUGE - TOP	48 RUDDER CONTROLS
11 FUEL FILTER - TOP	29 AILERON CONTROL & DINGHY RELEASE	49 CONNECTING BOLTS
12 FUEL TANK STRAPS	30 FUEL PUMP FILTER	50 AERIAL TENSION SPRING
13 FUEL LEVEL GAUGE - TOP	31 REFUELLING ELBOW - TOP	51 RUDDER TRIMMER & CONNECTING BOLTS
14 REFUELLING ELBOW - TOP	32 FUEL PUMP - TOP	52 AERIAL PULLEY
15 FUEL PUMP - TOP	33 AIRSCREW DE-ICING - TOP	53 RUDDER CONTROLS TOP & BOTTOM
16 FUEL PUMP FILTER	34 REFUELLING CONNECTION - TOP	54 RUDDER HINGE CUFFS
17 AILERON CONTROL	35 AIR VENT - TOP	55 HINGE BOLTS
18 AILERON CONTROL ARM	36 FUEL LEVEL GAUGE - TOP	56 FAIRLEAD
	37 FUEL FILLER - TOP	
	38 EXTRA REFUELLING ELBOW - TOP (WHEN REQUIRED)	

ACCESS & INSPECTION PANELS

ALL PANELS ARE IN THE BOTTOM SKIN EXCEPT WHERE STATED OTHERWISE

FIG 30

ABOVE Positions of Lancaster access and inspection panels.
(Crown Copyright)

Servicing a Lancaster

The servicing cycle of the BBMF Lancaster is eight years between majors. This is worked out according to the hours flown, the fatigue life of the airframe, components that are fitted, known structural failures and the risks of flying a 60-plus-year-old aircraft. All these factors are considered and a schedule is produced. This schedule not only takes into consideration the aircraft itself but also the parts in it which have their own specific lifespan, either in flying hours, landings or calendar time. For example, a main wheel is lifed for 100 landings, so this would have to be removed and serviced regardless of whether the aircraft itself was due a service.

Because of the size of the aircraft the flight servicing is carried out by the individual trades: airframe, engine, and electrics. When servicings have been completed they're signed for on the appropriate document, form F705, in the aircraft flight log form F700. This form is then signed by the pilot to acknowledge he accepts that the aircraft is ready for flight.

Before Flight Servicing

This is carried out within 24 hours of the aircraft's scheduled take-off time. If the aircraft doesn't fly within that period then the service has to be repeated. The following items are checked:

1 Internal and external checks to ensure all panels are secure.
2 Check of all the flying controls to make sure they're in working order and free of all restrictions.
3 Tyre pressures are checked.
4 All Plexiglas is checked and cleaned.
5 Crew harnesses are checked.
6 Oil, coolant, pneumatic and hydraulic fluids are checked to ensure they're at the correct level and are replenished if necessary.
7 The aircraft is refuelled to the required level.
8 The electrical systems are checked, *eg* the navigation lights.
9 Engine controls are checked for restrictions.

After Flight Servicing

Valid for seven days, this is carried out as soon as possible after landing to ensure that any problems that are identified can be corrected before the aircraft flies again. Such problems may include worn tyres, broken fasteners and oil leaks. The ground crew will:

1 Refuel the aircraft.
2 Clean the exterior to maintain the aircraft in display condition.
3 Tidy the aircrew harnesses.
4 Carry out a visual inspection, looking for cracks and damage such as exhaust stubs that have holed and loose screws or panel fasteners.

Turnaround Servicing

This is carried out if the aircraft is scheduled to fly again within a few hours of landing, and involves the following:

1 Refuel the aircraft as necessary.
2 Clean the windscreen and canopy.
3 A quick visual check of the exterior of the aircraft.

Oils and pressures aren't checked during this servicing, as everything is too hot.

Lubricants and fluids

- **Fuel** – Avgas F18 100LL, 2,154 gallons (however, PA474 flies with between 600 and 1,000 gallons).
- **Oil** – OM270-Aeroshell 100, 150 gallons.
- **Hydraulic fluid** – OM15/H515.
- **Coolant** – AL3.
- **Lubricating oil** – OM150, used for hinges and bearings.

ABOVE With the fuel bowser in position and the boom extended, refuelling begins.
(Paul Blackah/ Crown Copyright)

LEFT Corporal Crosby refuelling the number 1 port fuel tank.
(Paul Blackah/ Crown Copyright)

**RIGHT Wheel
retraction sequence.**
(Jarrod Cotter)

Primary Servicing

This service is carried out at 56 hours' flying time or thereabouts. Requiring about five technicians and taking two to three days, it consists of an inspection of the airframe and engines for general wear and tear:

1 Flying controls are inspected and lubricated.
2 The undercarriage is inspected and lubricated.
3 Engine filters are removed and checked for debris. A soap sample is taken to check for any contaminant in the oil.
4 The oil tanks are drained and oil is changed.
5 The magneto contact breaker points are checked to ensure that they're set correctly.

Annual Servicing

This is carried out at 112 flying hours or annually, whichever comes first. It usually starts at the end of the display season and takes approximately six months to complete. It includes everything carried out during primary servicing plus the following:

1 The internal and external structure of the aircraft is inspected for cracks and corrosion.
2 X-rays are taken of the rudders, fins, flaps and mainplanes.
3 Wheels are removed and serviced.
4 Brake units are inspected and tested.
5 Flying control runs are inspected.
6 Flying controls are inspected, rigged and a range of movements carried out.
7 Undercarriage hydraulic components are inspected and an emergency blow-down check is carried out.
8 Undercarriage and brake functions tests are carried out.
9 The engines are inspected and serviced.
10 Oil and coolant are replaced.
11 Propellers are inspected.
12 Electrical systems and instruments are checked.
13 Compass swing is carried out.

At the end of the annual service the aircraft is put through a series of engine ground runs. Once these are completed satisfactorily it is then air tested.

ABOVE **Engineers working on the number 3 engine.** *(Crown Copyright)*

Minor Servicing

This is carried out every four years and is basically an annual service plus:

1 The wing joining bolts are removed and inspected.
2 Wing plug rivets are removed, holes are inspected and rivets are replaced. (British Aerospace personnel are responsible for this task.)
3 Instruments are removed, serviced and refitted.

Major Servicing

Carried out every eight years by an outside agency, who will tender for the contract. This is a much more in-depth service which includes all the work carried out during the Annual and Minor services plus:

1 Flying controls are removed and fabric is replaced on the ailerons.
2 Undercarriage is removed and overhauled.
3 Fuel tanks are removed and overhauled.
4 Engines are removed to allow for the engine bearers to be removed for non-destructive testing and inspection.
5 Oil tanks are removed and overhauled.
6 Radiators and oil coolers are removed for overhaul.
7 Propellers are removed for inspection.
8 All hydraulic and pneumatic components are removed for overhaul.
9 Flying control cables and engine control cables are removed and inspected.

The opportunity is also taken to repaint the aircraft. Depending on the condition of the paintwork when it arrives for its service, the aircraft is either stripped to bare metal or the paintwork is simply scuffed to accept new paint.

Engine ground runs and air testing are carried out once the service is complete.

Common faults

Common faults with the Lancaster include minor oil and coolant leaks, which are generally rectified by tightening jubilee clips on rubber hoses. If this doesn't solve the problem new pipes will be manufactured and fitted.

Fabric tapes that cover the transportation joints and various seams on the aircraft often peel back and have to be replaced using new tape and dope.

Loose rivets require replacing and regular checks are carried out to locate any areas that require attention.

Brake bags overheat and lose their pressure so require replacement. Although this is not a major job, if the problem should occur when the aircraft is away from base it requires a lorry carrying a 25-tonne jack, a wheel chariot, wing trestles, a crane and additional ground crew.

NDT – non-destructive testing

There are four methods of non-destructive testing carried out on the Lancaster: X-rays, ultrasound, magnetic particle and dye penetrant.

The X-ray checks are carried out to examine parts or areas on the Lancaster that can't be easily accessed, such as the fins, flaps and engine bearers. The X-ray check will usually show up any internal corrosion or cracking.

The ultrasound check uses sound waves to detect cracking around the bore of a hole. To do this a probe is inserted into the hole – for example, the wing joint shackle holes – and a meter reading indicates if there is any sign of damage around it.

Magnetic particle checks are used to look for cracks in ferrous metal components. The component is painted with a fluid containing iron filings and an electric current is passed through it. The sample is then examined under ultra-violet light, which will highlight any faults that are present. Afterwards the sample is de-magnetised.

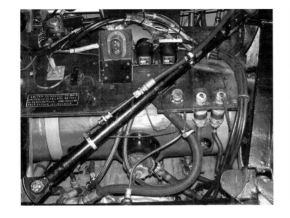

Dye penetrant checks are used to look for cracks in both ferrous and non-ferrous components. The component is painted with a fluorescent purple dye, cleaned, and then sprayed with a white developer, which, after approximately 40 minutes, will highlight any cracks. These show up as fine purple lines.

Keeping records

The BBMF Lancaster is operated using a Form 700. This log records the aircraft's flying hours, landings, and any faults that occur. The forms that log the aircraft's flying hours (F724) and faults (F707A) are permanently retained by the BBMF, whilst any other paperwork, such as that for Major or Primary services, is kept for eight years and then disposed of.

Engines and propellers have their own log cards, which stay with the particular component. These detail dates of fitment, when an item is due for an overhaul, and what repairs have been carried out.

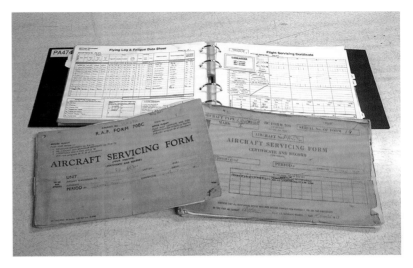

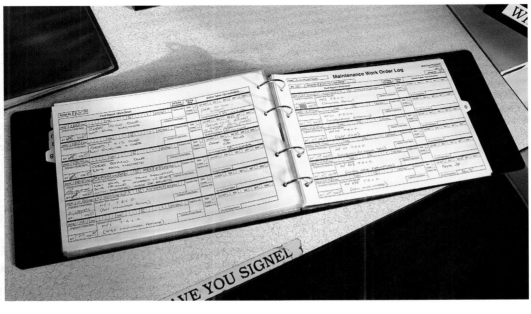

RIGHT Number 3 engine with all the cowlings removed, revealing various components not normally seen, the most obvious being the radiator. *(Jarrod Cotter)*

Picking a new colour scheme

Every time PA474 undergoes a Major servicing the BBMF changes its squadron codes to reflect a specific aircraft that flew on operations during World War Two. Once the choice is made research is carried out to find information on that specific aircraft's crew members and missions, and to collect as many photographs as possible to ensure that the finished markings and codes are accurate.

The BBMF is always grateful for the general public's response when help is requested in achieving this.

BELOW When all the flying's done, it's down to the engineers to carry out an after-flight inspection and then carefully put the Lancaster away in the safety of the BBMF's hangar. *(Jarrod Cotter)*

Heroes without wings

Although it is aircrew stories that we read about most, the vital work of the RAF's wartime ground crews should never be overlooked. It is sobering to note that around 8,000 men and women of Bomber Command were killed in the UK while carrying out their various ground-based duties, often under dangerous and trying conditions. Not the least of these was working round the clock in the open air on exposed airfields, often in the extreme cold and wet of British winters. Many suffered ill health as a result of this constant exposure to the elements, and some became chronically ill.

Try and imagine your fingers numb with cold, fumbling with frozen nuts and bolts, pipe work and engine cowlings, while standing on a raised scaffolding platform at engine height as a blizzard of snow or sleet sweeps around you. You blow on your hands and stamp your feet, trying hard to get some circulation back into them. You can't just leave the job till later: 'ops' are on tonight…

Through the following extracts we get an insight into the work of a Lancaster's ground crew, and their close relationships with the aircrew – who respected them enormously.

Stan Wells, groundcrew, No 626 Squadron, RAF Wickenby, Lincolnshire

'We really loved our own allotted Lanc. She was fussed over like a new car, though we did not always get a brand new machine fresh from the factory. She was as much ours, of course, as the aircrew to whom she was assigned. She was swept and cleaned inside, and woe betide anyone who left a cigarette end around or was sick and said nothing.

'Naturally, the enemy sometimes took a hand. If a kite came back from ops peppered with holes and jagged edges, we would jokingly curse the aircrew for not being more careful!

'It was a proud boast to start the engines first time, regardless of the weather. However, a snag such as a sudden mag drop could not be helped. The Squadron Engineering Officer and "Chiefy" were always on hand to help sort out a ticklish problem. Tools were in short supply

but we improvised and some ingenious concoctions resulted.

'Patching and replacing parts would mean a long toil, and many were the times we worked day and night without a break, for it was a matter of pride to get one's kite back in the line as quickly as possible. The weather was perhaps our biggest enemy; soaked to the skin or blue with cold, we would be kept going with constant mugs of piping hot tea, brewed on our own stove.

'Relations with the aircrews were excellent. During their tour of ops we got to know a crew very well. Often we would play cricket, football or have a round or two at cards over a brew-up at the hut when take-off was delayed. This was particularly so during the summer and autumn of 1944, when the second front opened and the daylight trips began in earnest.

'In the dark grim days of 1943, with the Battle of the Ruhr in full swing, and again over the winter of 1943–4 – the Battle of Berlin – losses were heavy and few crews got past ten trips. Some were unlucky, going down on the last five. When a crew did not return there would be glum faces, but within a day or two a new crew would arrive and the whole cycle would begin again.

'Once a kite was airborne we would take it in turns to wait up for her, and always there would be some of us to greet the crew when they returned. After each operation we would proudly paint a bomb symbol with a stencil up on the kite's nose, and much friendly competition existed as to who had the kite with the most ops.'

Extract from *Lancaster at War* by Mike Garbett and Brian Goulding (Ian Allan, 1971)

ABOVE Wartime engineers work hard on numbers 3 and 4 engines to prepare a Lancaster for its next night of operations. *(RAF Museum)*

Cliff Allan, groundcrew, No 467 Squadron, RAF Bottesford, Leicestershire

'A parade of flight personnel at the MT [motor transport] section followed breakfast, and then it was all aboard for the dispersals in a fog, thickening fast.

'Lancaster "H-Harry" loomed ahead, immobile and inoffensive, as the truck drew near and skidded to a halt. Reluctantly her ground crew dropped on to the crackling dispersal pan, the truck moved off and "H-Harry" was swallowed up by the dark curtain swirling behind. The call "G-George" drifted back from the cab and we knew we had arrived at our charge. "George" stood completely covered in white hoar frost; from each airscrew hung a two-inch wide icicle leading to the ground, and tapes holding engine and turret covers were frozen solid. "Dusty" Coleman, our rigger, found the door into the aircraft welded tight with the frost and disappeared into the fog to report. All the aircraft of No 467 Squadron were enveloped in the deep freeze and, no doubt, so was all 5 Group.

'It was a great relief on days like these to complete the DIs [daily inspections] without snags, but this was not always the case. One such day followed a pilot reporting an airscrew that did not respond between coarse and fine pitch. After the DIs, the engine with the faulty prop was test run and shut down. Jack, our Aussie corporal, went through all the possible faults but could find nothing amiss; so, by agreement with Laurie Parker [sergeant], made the decision to change the prop.

'It was not a long job to fit a new one, but nonetheless a frustrating task assembling the necessary equipment. Requisitions for replacements were left in our corporal's capable hands, and two of us joined him for a trip back to the maintenance hangar. There he hunted down a new prop whilst we commandeered a portable hand-crane.

'The sky had been very grey and overcast, and a slight flurry of snow looked ominous. The spinner was removed, the rope sling attached to the old prop, and the large hub loosened to allow the oil to be drained off; then the hand-crane was brought into use.

'Everything was going smoothly when, just as if someone had turned a switch, down came the snow thick and heavy. Unperturbed, we carried on, swinging the prop away and on to the edge of dispersal. By the time the new prop was cranked into the air a blizzard was raging and, though only a few yards from the engine, we couldn't see it for the blinding snow. The quick decision to abandon any further attempts was unanimous and on hurriedly applying covers we retreated to our shack. This was one of the rare occasions when we had to submit to the weather and continue the following day.'

Frank Hawkins, armourer, No 9 Squadron, RAF Bardney, Lincolnshire

'Our day would normally commence with daily inspections, when the armourers would visit their designated kites and go through the procedure of checking guns, turrets, bomb gear, etc. These DIs were very thorough as the squadron – indeed Bomber Command in general – had, during the winter of 1943–4 in particular, experienced above average trouble with gun stoppages (usually attributed to icing). While icing may well have been a contributory factor, Maguire [Pilot Officer, Squadron Armament Officer] was of the opinion that the answer lay in the fact that the armament staff on many stations were overwhelmed; the monumental task of preparing and handling vast quantities of bombs and incendiaries every day meant that other aspects tended to "go to the wall". It was always maximum effort and a month of continuous operations was a shattering experience; and month followed month with only a quick breather in between.

'All the armament staff at Bardney were, during the winter of 1943–4, either fully or partially employed in the handling and preparation of bombs; no one was immune – except perhaps for the WAAF on the ammunition belting section. All armourers could expect to be, and often were, diverted from their normal duties to back up the hard-pressed teams in the bomb dump and under the aircraft.'

Extracts from *Lancaster at War 2* by Mike Garbett and Brian Goulding (Ian Allan, 1984)

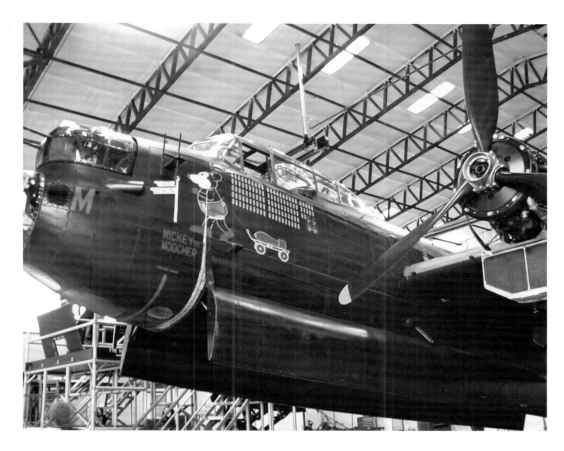

LEFT The engine cowlings and spinners have been removed. Note the nose section joint fabric tape has also been removed. The aircraft is being prepared for paint stripping. *(Bruce Irvine)*

From Mickey to the Phantom

During the winter of 2006/7 the BBMF Lancaster underwent a Major service. The contract for this was awarded by the Nimrod Integrated Project Team, which manages the Battle of Britain Memorial Flight. Bruce Irvine from Classic Aircraft Maintenance Ltd, the Project Manager, tells his side of the story:

'The ad in the *EU Journal* was simple: "The MoD have a requirement to carry out Major maintenance on BBMF Lancaster PA474 during Winter 2006/07. Interested parties should contact the Nimrod IPT, DLO (now DE&S), RAF Wyton." After a complex competitive tendering process the contract was awarded to Atlantic Airmotive, the engineering section of Air Atlantique's Classic Flight.

'The previous Major was carried out in 1999 at RAF St Athan by RAF personnel, and although the tradesmen of the Classic Flight were experienced on large aircraft such as the

Dakota and Shackleton this Major saw a team of entirely civilian contractors carrying out the work to a new maintenance schedule, so there would be no previous experience to fall back on. The condition of the aircraft looked sound,

BELOW The paint removal is complete, leaving the aircraft with a bare metal finish. *(Bruce Irvine)*

ABOVE The aircraft is jacked and trestled. All the engines, engine bearer frames and undercarriage legs have been removed. *(Bruce Irvine)*

BELOW The rear fuselage is separated from the rest of the aircraft to allow the removal of the rudder and elevator control rod runs. *(Bruce Irvine)*

but as with any project of this size and nature of work, it could not be taken for granted that there wouldn't be any surprises as the paint, panels and various components were removed.

'The work identified as "Major Maintenance" is detailed in an Air Publication and is the core tasking. Additional tasking was also identified at the initial tendering stage; what could not be identified, initially, would be the rectification tasks. As these tasks arise they must be identified and scoped and then authorised by the MoD representative before work can commence. This meant constant liaison with the MoD to ensure that the work being carried out was required and was carried out to the highest standards.

'It was decided that the best way to tackle the job was to divide the workload into two parts. As the Project Manager I would lead the project for the contractor, be responsible for the control and overall co-ordination and also be the link with the Engineering Authority (DE&S) from RAF Wyton, who had overall responsibility for the aircraft. The physical hands-on aspects, however, would be the responsibility of Atlantique's Classic Flight Chief Engineer, Ben Cox.

'This would allow Ben to concentrate on the day-to-day tasks and allow me to focus on supporting his activities, whilst working in conjunction with the DE&S engineer (Chief Technician Colin Robertson) to keep the aircraft on course for its output date whilst ensuring that the appropriate level of rectification was being carried out. The Major would then be divided into phases: initial inspection and removals, detailed inspections, repair and rectification, refit, and finally functional testing.

'The initial timeframe to carry out the Major was approximately six months. To make sure this deadline was achieved it was decided that the best way to perform the maintenance was to keep the airframe work in-house but to subcontract the bay maintenance items, for example the hydraulic and pneumatic components.

'The contract also required the aircraft to be stripped to bare metal and resprayed. This would also be carried out by a subcontractor. At any one time over 100 tradesmen would be working on the aircraft or its various parts. With so many different subcontractors and precise deadlines, the control of the project was no mean feat in itself.

'The Lancaster arrived at Coventry Airport on 2 October 2006 to a large crowd of both public and media. Somehow the story had leaked out and it appeared that all the surrounding roads leading to or running next to the airport were full of cars waiting for the aircraft. On arrival the bomber flew a circuit, which gave the crowds something for their patience. After taxiing to the required slot, where again there was much media in attendance, the crew disembarked and carried out the necessary paperwork. *Mickey the Moocher* made its last public appearance as it was towed into Air Atlantique's hangar, where it would stay for the next six months or so.

'As the aircraft was to be stripped back to bare metal the decision was taken to carry this out as soon as possible. This would allow the inspections for surface corrosion to be carried out early into the servicing, giving us time to make any repairs if required. However, before stripping could commence the propellers and the engines had to be removed. They could have remained in situ for the strip, but as they

ABOVE Work being carried out on the engine bay rear bulkhead. *(Bruce Irvine)*

were coming off anyway this was the best time to do it, as it reduced any risk of contaminating the engine bays or paint-stripper damage to the propellers.

'With the spinners removed, access was gained to the hub bolts and the props were removed using a crane. As the props had

LEFT Inspected and repainted, the engine bearers are refitted. The red item behind the bulkhead is the engine oil tank. *(Bruce Irvine)*

ABOVE **Engine refit in progress.** (Bruce Irvine)

been overhauled the previous year all that was required for these was a simple inspection.

'The RAF policy on Merlin engines is to "life" the engines at 500 hours, after which they're completely overhauled. On this occasion all four were still within life, so only some simple "top end" maintenance was required. This was carried out by BBMF tradesmen. Removal of the engines took several days as many of the ancillary components had to be removed or disconnected before the engines themselves could be taken off. At this stage it was important to ensure that everything was labelled correctly and the use of digital cameras became second nature to ensure the correct refitting of components.

'All copper pipe work had to be heat treated, as the copper hardens through ageing. Each pipe or pipe assembly had to be removed and labelled in such a way that it would still be identifiable after it had been in a furnace for several hours to anneal the metal.

'The next big job was the bare-metal strip. This was carried out by a specialist aircraft painting company called Sprayavia, which is based at Norwich Airport. The aircraft was surrounded by scaffolding to provide a safe working platform. Transparencies were masked with three different layers of protection, then a chemical stripper was applied to the main areas of the aircraft. The stripper and paint were then removed using water. However, in some areas the only option was to rub down by

hand – a long and laborious job. The paint strip took a team of six painters some ten days to complete.

'When the aircraft was finally down to bare metal and the staging removed from around it, the job of carrying out detailed inspection of all the surfaces began. A little corrosion was found in various locations, but the surfaces were generally in very good condition and little remedial work, other than that already identified, was required. One area which had previously been identified as 'Additional Work' to the core tasking and in need of attention was the starboard wingtip.

'During the previous winter maintenance the port wingtip had been found to be corroded, and although the starboard looked in good condition it was thought that a little time investigating the tip after it had been stripped of its paint would be useful. It proved to be the correct thing to do. The leading edge was corroded and a repair to the upper surface was also showing signs of corrosion. The wingtip was removed to allow ease of access, the upper surface skin was replaced, and the corrosion on the leading edges dressed and repaired.

'Another area that was brought to our attention was that of the rear panel of the port bomb door. A stainless steel skin had replaced the original alloy skin and it was thought that this had been fitted over the old alloy during one of the various trial fits that the aircraft had undergone in the 1950/60s. The steel skin was removed to reveal what was expected: a badly corroded existing alloy skin. This was removed and the stringers and frames below it were inspected – fortunately they were found to be in good condition. This was a bonus, as trying to find or remanufacture these stringers and frames could have proved time-consuming.

'As the detailed inspections progressed more and more components were removed from the aircraft for bay maintenance or to allow for deep inspection. As the flaps were removed an inspection of the flap operating tubes revealed one of the aspects of the task we had all feared – a major component failure.

'The operating tubes on the starboard side were found to be corroded and in one specific area a crack had appeared. The DE&S engineer was informed immediately the problem was discovered and, after discussing various options, it was agreed that the only option open to us was to remove and replace the tubes – but we were 99 per cent certain that no spare tubes existed, and even if they did they could be as corroded as the ones fitted. A check of the spares held at RAF Coningsby confirmed our fears; new control tubes would have to be made.

'The tubes were removed and dispatched to Retro Track and Air based in Dursley who took on the task to remanufacture. But there would be a penalty, as this would take time. Tubing of this size would have to be specially milled

and there was nowhere in the UK that could provide the diameter, wall thickness and lengths required, so it would have to be sourced outside the UK. The tube also contained inserts that were fixed inside the tube and served as the mounting point for the connecting rods; these would also have to be remanufactured. This would all take approximately 16 weeks, and in a project such as this time was the one thing that we didn't have.

'The inspections and removals continued with no further great surprises other than finding some cracking on the engine frame welds. The frames were removed and repairs carried out by Skycraft, who did a really great job returning the

ABOVE Engine systems pipe work and electrical cables are refitted to the engine bearer. *(Bruce Irvine)*

LEFT The inboard engine is now complete with radiator and oil cooler. *(Bruce Irvine)*

frames well before the engine refit was planned.

'One of the additional requirements during the Major was the removal and replacement of the elevator and rudder flying control rods. These rods run the entire length of the port side and transmit the pilot's operation of the control column to the relevant control surfaces. They had been "snagged" earlier as showing initial signs of wear where they run through bearings housed in the various frames of the fuselage, and would have to be replaced.

'During the manufacturing stage of the aircraft these control rods are normally added as each section is being constructed, so the only way to remove them would be to take the fuselage apart. Through discussion with BAE Systems, the BBMF and DE&S, it was suggested that we might be able to take the nose off and withdraw the rods that way, but after inspecting the control rod run, with various components now removed, we discovered that; (a) the rivets that held the rod male and female end fittings, which linked all the rods together, would not go through the bearings; and (b) there was a slight deviation from a straight line that would not allow the rods to be taken out through the nose section. So that approach wasn't feasible.

'The alternative was to split the aircraft at each transport joint. This would allow easy access to the control rods for both removal and replacement but would take considerable time. The simplest way was to split the aircraft at the rear fuselage transport joint, as it had been some four years previously. The bolts would be relatively new, making the split easier, and we had sufficient trestles to support the aircraft.

'Splitting the aircraft at the rear fuselage joint still meant removing the rods through the bearings, which we knew wouldn't work. The rods would still have to have the end fittings taken off inside the aircraft before removal and then refitted after the rod had gone through the bearing. Although a lengthy process this was the best way to proceed, as it provided the least risk to the project. The idea of splitting the aircraft at the rear transport joint was put forward to the DE&S engineer and BAE Systems and, with both in agreement, we were given the green light to go ahead.

'Splitting the aircraft was relatively simple. It was jacked up to its level position using jacks under the mainplanes. An eye-bolt fitted to the tail section was then attached to a crane by a sling and the tail section was raised to the level position. A trestle was then positioned under the aircraft and the tail section rested upon it. Two more trestles were positioned either side of the rear section transport joint and the work of removing the bolts began. They were slowly removed until the final one came out with no more than a slight tap. The rear section was then simply pushed away from the main fuselage, giving us ample access to remove the control rods.

'This proved to be the easy part, as it then took nearly three weeks to remove and replace the existing rods, with each one having to have the end pieces removed in situ. The old rod was then removed from the aircraft by sliding it through numerous bearings, a new rod was cut to the exact length, the old bearings were replaced, the rod was slid back in and the end pieces were fitted.

'The wear characteristics of the rudder and elevator control rods also made us question the possibility of wear in the aileron control rods, as these are of the same construction, and upon further detailed examination we found similar wear characteristics just beginning. Our findings were put to the DE&S engineer, who agreed that the rods should be replaced. Luckily, at this point the flap and trailing edge of the wing had been removed, allowing easier access, so replacing the rods was an easy option to take.

BELOW A view of the port inner engine fitted to the bearer assembly. *(Bruce Irvine)*

'With the Lancaster now on jacks the undercarriage could be removed for bay maintenance. The removal itself proved simple enough, but when the legs were taken to the bay and stripped down some internal damage was discovered. No spare parts were available to replace the unserviceable components and the only option open to us to meet the timescale was to use the serviceable components from each panel to make up one serviceable leg. Fortunately a spare panel assembly (one complete leg unit) was available from the BMFF, but as this had been in storage for some time it was agreed that it should be inspected prior to fitting. Luckily everything was found to be serviceable, and between the removed legs and the spare we were able to provide a complete undercarriage.

'As late autumn gave way to winter the work in the hangar changed from inspection and removal to rectification. Loose rivets, worn anchor nuts, minor corrosion and cosmetic skin replacements were the order of the day, with the sound of air drills whizzing in the background replaced by the *prappt* of a rivet gun and block.

'Other than the ones mentioned above, no major rectification tasks were required. It was good to see the aircraft in such a good condition – a real testament to the tradesmen and women at the BBMF who regularly service the aircraft and to those who'd carried out Major maintenance in the past. It gave us the confidence that the maintenance schedules

used for the past 60 years really worked, and with the aircraft in such a good condition, with some 5,000 flying hours on the clock, it should be good for at least the same again.

'By January 2007 many of the components that had been sent for bay maintenance were beginning to return and could start to be refitted. Cockpit instruments, hydraulic components and undercarriage legs all had a new lease of life, and internally the aircraft was taking shape too. The extra control rods for the ailerons had arrived and had been fitted as far as possible. The fuselage had gone back together as easily as it had come apart and the new control rods for the rudder and elevator were in place and felt smooth and precise. The

ABOVE The aircraft is off its jacks. Fabric tapes have been applied to all the transportation joints before the aircraft is primed. *(Bruce Irvine)*

BELOW After the primer has been applied the aircraft is masked ready for application of the camouflage paintwork. *(Bruce Irvine)*

flap-operating tubes remained the one thing outside our control, outside anyone's control really, as the tubes had to be specially milled and it just took time. The tube inserts were ready and we just had to wait.

'There was still plenty to do on the fuel tanks, engine bearers had to be fitted and then the engines themselves had to be installed with all their accessories and ancillaries. The idea of going into repaint at this stage was debated, but some sections of the aircraft could not be painted, as the trailing edge was still off, awaiting the flap tubes. Although it would have been very unlikely, painting the aircraft at this stage could have resulted in a slight colour distortion and no one wanted anything but a perfect finish, as the first event the Lancaster was scheduled for was a commemoration ceremony at RAF Coningsby for the two units the new paint scheme would represent – 100 and 550 Squadrons.

'Finally the call came that the tubes were ready and could be picked up, which was done as soon as possible, and just four hours later they were being readied to be fitted. With the tubes in place the wing trailing edge could then be fitted and the vital repaint commenced.

'The repaint took a team of ten painters two weeks to complete, turning what was a rather strange looking aircraft back into one of the most distinctive in UK skies today. The black, or night, underside, with camouflage green and dark earth upper surfaces, have remained constant throughout the Lancaster's

life with the BBMF. However, with each Major maintenance the nose-art changes. In this case it changed from an affable *Mickey the Moocher* to the *Phantom of the Ruhr*, a distinct change to a far more sinister scheme. Nonetheless, the nose-art is fantastic and I must thank Sprayavia for their considerable input and patience in achieving the final result.

'With the paintwork complete we were able to get back to work on completing the installation of the engines and the final few components. Although no final output date had been given, a launch for the BBMF's 50th anniversary was planned for late April and we realised what an important point in the Flight's history this was. Not to have the Lancaster there in its new squadron colours would be unforgivable.

'As the date for the ceremony grew closer and closer we realised that the tempo in the hangar would have to be increased if we were going to get the aircraft out on time. At this stage 12-hour days and seven-day weeks were not uncommon. Although the MoD didn't push us, and safety was paramount, professionalism and a pride of being part of something great forced us to put in the hours to get the aircraft out on time.

'Slowly it was coming back together. The paint scheme was complete, including the nose-art, all instruments were refitted and the hydraulic components were in place. The undercarriage units had been refitted, as had the engines and propellers, so hydraulically and electrically the aircraft was sound; but the proof

RIGHT When the camouflage has been applied the markings are added. Here the roundel is going through this process.
(Bruce Irvine)

of the pudding was in the eating. "Electrics going on" – no sparks, no bangs, nothing, a good sign. "Hydraulics going on" – again nothing, another good sign.

'As the various hydraulic system function tests were completed the aircraft could be lowered off jacks and back onto the ground, a position it hadn't been in for over six months. As the flying controls range of movement checks were completed the next moment of truth came upon us: engine ground runs.

'The RAF is quite stringent as to who can run the engines on their aircraft. This is not just for commercial contractors but for all tradesmen, including their own, and a great amount of time, effort, training and care is taken before someone is authorised for ground runs. Doubly so with the Lancaster. There are very few people in the country, if not the world, who can safely fire up all four Merlin engines with confidence, so it was the tradesmen of the BBMF who carried out the ground runs.

'The engines were primed and finally the aircraft was towed out of the hangar into a beautiful sunny April morning. The Coventry Airport fire service had been informed and a fire tender had been dispatched to be in attendance should anything go wrong. A crowd slowly gathered. Although we hadn't realised, it was about lunchtime, so many airport workers were in a position to watch the aircraft as it began the final phase of the journey that would bring it back life.

'"Number 1 contact, contact." Slowly the propeller turned and after few rotations the Merlin roared into life, accelerated, and then steadied. Contact number 2, the same process, and so on up to number 4. Then all four Merlins were roaring outside the hangar, much to the joy of the onlookers and to us. This initial low power run had to be right otherwise we could be looking at an engine change and delaying the output date. Low power runs completed, high power runs were required. This meant the aircraft would have to go to the other side of the airport. During the high power runs a slight "mag drop" problem occurred, but by the following day this had been rectified and ground runs carried out again successfully. The Lancaster was now ready for its final test – the air test.

'Disaster! The following morning, as we entered the hangar to prep the aircraft for its test, a drop of fuel landed on the head of one of the maintenance team as he walked under the wing. Removing the panel below the fuel tank revealed what we had thought – a leak. The tank was removed to investigate further in the hope that it might be a union or fitting that was leaking. But that was not the case. It was the tank itself.

'The DE&S engineer was informed immediately, as this could have a serious impact on the output of the aircraft and the ability to carry out the air test. There were two options available: not to refit the tank, and get it repaired; or refit it, raise the appropriate paperwork to inform the aircrew and the ground crew, and carry on with the air test. Much discussion took place over the merits of both options between the contractor, the DE&S engineer, the BBMF ground crew and us. In the end the decision lay with the MoD, and the decision was to refit the tank. This was done, and by the time the aircrew arrived the panel was back on and the paperwork sorted.

'The aircraft was towed out into the daylight and again a large crowd had assembled both inside the airport site and outside the perimeter fence to see it fly. The engines were started up without any problems and the aircraft taxied off to the end of the runway after further engine checks.

'From where we stood we could see the aircraft start making its, what seemed painfully slow, run along the runway. Slowly the tail lifted into the air and a minute or so later the main wheels cleared the runway. As the aircraft started the climb we saw the undercarriage retract and the doors close. The Lancaster then banked to the right and headed off to carry out the air test.

'"If it's back in five minutes it's failed," was one comment, but five minutes led to ten, then to 20 and 30, and after about 40 minutes we were informed that PA474 was making its approach. As the bomber roared overhead we realised that everything must have gone well, though there might be some minor snags to sort. As we watched the undercarriage come down and the aircraft slowly descend through the sky I held my breath, waiting for touchdown and for the brakes to operate. As the aircraft taxied back into the slot it had left some 45 minutes earlier I let out a great sigh of relief.

'The engines stopped and the crew emerged. As we suspected, there were a couple of minor snags that were quick fixes, and a minor oil leak that was also soon sorted. Some hydraulic fluid had been seen very slowly leaking from one of the main oleos, and at first we thought this was merely the aircraft settling but it continued to weep, albeit very slowly. The

jobs we could carry out were completed and some other snags were addressed, but the aircrew were happy to take the aircraft back to RAF Coningsby. So as the evening started to draw to a close PA474 took off from Coventry Airport once again, this time not to return. After a magnificent flypast the aircraft banked to the right and flew home.

'After landing the leak from the oleo didn't stop, so the leg was removed and repaired. The leaking fuel tank was also replaced, and at the time of writing PA474 has flown over 100 hours during the 2007 flying season.

'My thanks go out to all those involved in this project. If I were to list everyone I'd be into another page, but special thanks go to Ben, Bob, Dan, John A, John and Paul – without your dedication this couldn't have been done. The tradesmen and women at the BBMF answered my questions on the phone and checked their stores system time and time again. Thanks too to Colin Robertson, whose open mindedness helped no end in getting over the problems we encountered, and to all the subcontractors I used to get the job finished with 36 hours to spare. Good project management, or just luck?'

BELOW PA474's repaint is finished and the major servicing is nearing completion. Engine ground runs are required and then the remaining cowlings and spinners can be refitted.
(Bruce Irvine)

Appendix 1

Part numbers

For ease of identification, each area of the Lancaster is designated a letter followed by the actual part number:

B – data and rigging
BBH – repairs
C – cockpit deck and fairings
D – fuselage structure
E – cowlings and fireproof bulkheads
F – wing structure
G – tailplane and elevators
H – fin and rudders
K – undercarriage, main and tail

N – furnishings
O – power plant
P – fuel and oil
Q – piping services, hydraulic and pneumatic
R – flying and trim controls
S – instrument and panels
T – radio and radar
U – ancillary equipment
V – electrical systems
W – bomb gear
X – gun gear
Z – sundries

The undercarriage legs and hydraulic components were all manufactured by Dowty, the wheels, brakes and pneumatic components by Dunlop, and the turrets by Fraser Nash. Each company operated its own numbering system. The Merlin engine has its own four or five-part number system prefixed by the letter D. A Packard Merlin is prefixed by the letters PD.

Dimensions and weights

All dimensions are with the Lancaster tail up:

Wingspan – 102ft
Length – 69ft 6in
Height – 20ft 6in
Tailplane span – 33ft

Maximum take-off weight (wartime) – 61,500lb
BBMF Lancaster – 48,000lb

Fuel – 2,154 gallons (the BBMF do not fill above 1,000 gallons maximum)
Oil tanks – 150 gallons
Main hydraulic system – 19½ gallons

PA474 avionics

Successive modifications have totally superseded the original avionics. The current equipment is as follows:

V/UHF – a PTR 1751 V/UHF radio.
VHF – an AD 120 VHF radio.
Intercom – an ARI 5388 intercom.
IFF – an ARI 23373/1 IFF system.

DME – DME, ARI 23414, installed under SRIM 4147 Part A.
VOR – a VOR system, installed under SRIM 4147 Part B.

PA474 general limitations

Weight limitations

The all-up take-off and landing weights are limited to a maximum of 48,000lb.

Centre of gravity limitations

The position of the centre of gravity is not to fall outside the following limits:
Aft: 60.6in aft of the datum.
Forward: 41in aft of the datum.

Speed limitations

The maximum speeds for operating the aircraft are to be as follows:
Diving – not to exceed 200 knots.
Undercarriage down – not to exceed 150 knots.
Flaps selected – not to exceed 150 knots.
Operation of bomb doors – not to exceed 150 knots.
All flying – not to exceed 200 knots.

Maximum permitted normal accelerations

Manoeuvres involving negative normal accelerations are not permitted. The following accelerometer readings, which include accelerations due to turbulence, are not to be exceeded:
Normal operation and displays – 1.5g.
Never exceed – 1.8g.

Stalling

Intentional stalling in accelerated flight is prohibited. The limitations regarding stalling laid down in the Aircrew Manual are to be observed.

Crosswind limitation

The maximum permissible crosswind component for take-off and landing is 15 knots.

PA474 engine limitations

The following engine limitations are never to be exceeded:

	rpm	Boost lb/sq in	Temperature °C Coolant	Oil
Max take-off to 1,000ft	3,000	+18*	135	105
Max climbing 1 hour limit	2,850	+9	125	90
Max continuous	2,650	+7	105	90
'Combat' 5 minutes limit	3,000	+18*	135	105

*+18 lb/sq in boost must not be used below 2,850rpm.

Under normal operating conditions, the following engine limitations are not to be exceeded:

	rpm	Boost lb/sq in	Temperature °C Coolant	Oil
Take-off (max)	3,000	+9	135	105
Take-off (normal)	3,000	+7	135	105
Max continuous	2,650	+7	105	90
Normal climb	2,400	+4	105	90
Cruise	1,900	+4	105	90

Descend at 150 knots at −2 to −4lb/sq in boost to attain 500ft/min rate of descent.

Maximum overspeed

The maximum permissible overspeed is 3,150rpm for 20 seconds.

Oil pressure

The oil pressure under normal conditions should remain between 60 and 80lb/sq in. The minimum permissible oil pressure is 30lb/sq in.

Minimum temperatures

The engines are not to be run at above 1,200rpm until the following minimum temperatures have been achieved:
Oil: +15°C.
Coolant: +40°C.

Appendix 2

Surviving Lancasters

Listed here are the 15 extant Lancasters which are currently on public display. Additionally Lancaster VII NX664 WU-21 is undergoing a comprehensive restoration at Le Bourget in Paris. Another Lancaster is stored dismantled in the USA and various cockpit sections (both original and mock-ups) also remain, including the Imperial War Museum Lambeth's Mark I DV372 *Old Fred*, which has been on public display since just after the end of World War Two.

	Mk	No	Location	Status
1	Mark I	R5868 *S-Sugar*	RAF Museum, London, Hendon, UK	Museum display
2	Mark I	W4783 *G-for-George*	Australian War Memorial, Canberra, ACT, Australia	Museum display
3	Mark X	FM104	Toronto Aerospace Museum, Ontario, Canada	Museum display
4	Mark X	FM136	Aero Space Museum, Calgary, Alberta, Canada	Museum display
5	Mark X	FM159	Nanton Lancaster Society and Air Museum, Nanton, Alberta, Canada	Museum display, engines being brought to running order
6	Mark X	FM212	Windsor, Ontario, Canada	Under restoration
7	Mark X	FM213 (C-GVRA)	Canadian Warplane Heritage Museum, Hamilton, Ontario, Canada	Fully airworthy
8	Mark X	KB839	Greenwood Military Aviation Museum, Nova Scotia, Canada	Museum display
9	Mark X	KB882	St Jacques Airport, Edmundston, New Brunswick, Canada.	Displayed
10	Mark X	KB889	Imperial War Museum, Duxford, Cambridgeshire, UK	Museum display
11	Mark X	KB944	Canada Aviation Museum, Ottawa, Ontario, Canada	Museum display
12	Mark VII	NX611 *Just Jane*	Lincolnshire Aviation Heritage Centre, East Kirkby, Lincolnshire, UK	Taxiiable
13	Mark VII	NX622	RAAF Association Aviation Heritage Museum, Bull Creek, Perth, Western Australia	Museum display
14	Mark VII	NX665	Museum of Transport and Technology, Austin, Auckland, New Zealand	Museum display
15	Mark I	PA474 *Phantom of the Ruhr*	Battle of Britain Memorial Flight, RAF Coningsby, Lincolnshire, UK	Fully airworthy

Appendix 3

Glossary and abbreviations

ADF – Automatic direction finder, a radio receiver that points to a selected transmitter.

AP – Armour-piercing bomb.

AS – Anti-submarine bomb.

BAe – British Aerospace.

BBMF – Battle of Britain Memorial Flight.

Boost – The pressure of the fuel/air mixture in the induction manifold of the engine. Measured in pounds per square inch on the boost gauge in the cockpit, this indicates the power level delivered by the engine.

CFS – Central Flying School.

CSU – Constant speed unit. This unit, fitted to the engine, automatically controls the engine rpm and the propeller pitch mechanism so that they operate at high efficiency over a wide range of flight conditions. The pilot sets the required engine rpm using his control lever, and a governor automatically controls the pitch of the propeller blades. Thus the aircraft flies at the most efficient value for the engine power selected and the speed of the aircraft.

DME – Distance measuring equipment; gives the distance to the transmitter.

F700 – Form 700 aircraft logbook.

FE – Far East (as in FE Standard).

GP – General purpose.

GPS – Global positioning system.

HC – High capacity bomb.

HE – High explosive bomb.

IFR – Instrument flight rules.

IMC – Instrument meteorological conditions.

IP – Initial point.

LC – Low capacity bomb.

LORAN C – Long-range aid to navigation level C.

Mass balance horn – A weight on the flying control surface that assists in its movement.

MC – Medium capacity bomb.

NOTAM – Notice to airmen. Advisory notice giving information on the establishment, condition or change in any aeronautical facility, service, procedure or hazard.

OC – Officer Commanding.

QFE – Airfield atmospheric pressure reading.

rpm – Revolutions per minute.

SAP – Semi-armour-piercing bomb.

SBC – Small bomb container.

SWG – Standard wire gauge.

Taboo arms – Exterior arms on the mid-upper turret, running around a track, that prevent the gunner from shooting off the tailplane.

THUM – Temperature and Humidity Flight.

TOT – Time on target.

Trim tab – A small control surface that, when set, enables the aircraft to fly straight and level without any forces on the control column.

U/C – Undercarriage.

USA bomb – A bomb manufactured in the USA.

VFR – Visual flight rules.

VMC – Visual meteorological conditions.

VOR – Very high frequency omni-directional radio range; a navigation aid.

Appendix 4

Useful addresses

Airframe Assemblies
Hangar 6S
Isle of Wight Airport
Sandown
Isle of Wight PO36 0JP
Tel 01983 408661/404462
Produces replacement airframe and wing components.

Anglia Radiators
Unit 4
Stanley Road
Cambridge CB5 8LB
Tel 01223 314444
Builds replacement radiators and oil coolers.

ARCo
Duxford Airfield
Cambridgeshire CB2 4QR
Tel 01223 835313
Maintenance on historic aircraft.

Classic Aircraft Maintenance Ltd
90 Conduit Rd
Stamford
Lincolnshire PE9 1QL
Maintenance on historic aircraft.

Dunlop Tyres
40 Fort Parkway
Erdington
Birmingham
West Midlands
B24 9HL

Hanley Smith
7 South Rd
Templefields
Harlow
Essex
CM20 2AP
Tel 01279 414446
Overhauls undercarriage legs.

Lincolnshire's Lancaster Association
PO Box 474
Lincoln
LN5 8ZW
Registered charity, supporting the
Battle of Britain Memorial Flight.

Ormonde Aircraft Ltd
Hangar 2
Nottingham Airport
Tollerton Lane
Nottingham NG12 4GA
Tel/Fax 01159 813343
Produces replacement airframe and wing
components.

Retro Track and Air
Upthorpe Iron Works
Upthorpe Lane
Dursley
Gloucestershire GL11 5HP
Tel 01453 545360
Overhauls engines.

Supermarine Aero Engineering Ltd
Mitchell Works
Steventon Place
Burslem
Stoke-on-Trent
Staffordshire ST6 4AS
Tel 01782 811344
Machine components.

Vintage Fabrics Ltd
Boones Farm
Helstead Road
High Garret
Braintree
Essex CM7 5PB
Tel 01376 550553
Fabric for the flying controls, rudder
and elevators.

Index

(Jarrod Cotter)

This book has hopefully given the reader an insight into the maintenance and flying of the sole remaining RAF Lancaster. But we must remember that all you have seen and read about is a commemoration of the more than 55,000 Bomber Command aircrew who never came home from operations. This is reflected on a plaque positioned just aft of PA474's main entrance. Each time the crew enter and leave the aircraft they pass the Bomber Command crest and the simple but extremely meaningful words:

'TO REMEMBER THE MANY'